A BOOK OF DEVOTIONS

getting a CLUE
in a clueless world

D0630961

Other books by Ross Campbell:

How to Really Love Your Child
How to Really Love Your Teenager
How to Really Know Your Child

Other books by Dave Lambert:

Jumper Fables (with Ken Davis)
Cybershock: Totally Wired
Celebrating Christmas as If It Matters

A BOOK OF DEVOTIONS

getting a CLUE

in a clueless world

Hope, Encouragement & Challenge
for Students

Dr. Ross Campbell & Dave Lambert

ZondervanPublishingHouse
Grand Rapids, Michigan

A Division of HarperCollinsPublishers

Getting a Clue in a Clueless World
Copyright © 1996 by David Lambert and Ross Campbell

Requests for information should be addressed to:

▦ ZondervanPublishingHouse
Grand Rapids, Michigan 49530

Library of Congress Cataloging-in-Publication Data

Campbell, Ross, 1936–
    Getting a clue in a clueless world : hope, encouragement, and challenge for
students / Ross Campbell and Dave Lambert
      p.   cm.
    Includes bibliographical references (p.)
    Summary: Presents sixty stories, accompanied by Bible verses, Scriptural
references, and exercises, that are meant to help teenagers deal with their lives
by strengthening their relationship with God.
    ISBN: 0-310-20817-3 (pbk. : alk. paper)
    1. Hope—Religious aspects—Christianity—Juvenile literature.
2. Encouragement—Religious aspects—Christianity—Juvenile literature.
3. Christian life—Juvenile literature.   4. Christian life—Biblical teaching—
Juvenile literature. [1. Christian life. 2. Conduct of life.]   I. Lambert,
David, 1948– .   II. Title.
BV4638.C24 1996
248.8'3-dc20   96-8621
                                                        CIP

Printed in the United States of America

---

96 97 98 99 00 01 02 03 / ❖ DH/ 10 9 8 7 6 5 4 3 2

This book is dedicated to all of the teens who have crossed paths with me over the years and who have taught me so much of what I know—and of what I'm trying to pass along in this book. Thank you.

—Ross

For Sarai, who by the time she was seventeen had experienced—and barely survived—more of life than most people three times her age, and had the scars and the wisdom to prove it. Stay strong.

—Dave

Read This First—or Else!

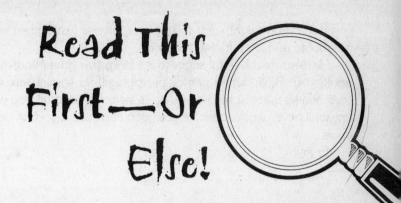

Or else what?

OK, we admit it. That was an empty threat.

BUT—this *is* important, and it'll only take you a minute to read.

First, about the names. We wrote this book together, and in it we tell a lot of stories. Some of the stories are things that happened to Ross, and some of them happened to Dave. That could be confusing if you don't know who the "I" in each story is, so after the title of most of the stories, you'll see a name—either Ross or Dave. That tells you who the "I" in that story is. If you don't see any name, that means it's not about something that happened to one of us.

Second, you can use this book any way you want—read one section a day or, if you're enjoying it, read more. It's up to you. But our suggestion is to read one section a day, because in each daily reading, we suggest something for you to try that day, and if you read several of them, you'll be less likely to try the experiments. And they can be helpful. Try it that way and see if you like it. And hey—if you get busy and skip a few days, don't feel guilty. Just get back to it as soon as you can.

Third, sometimes in this book, we'll ask you to make a list or write something down. You could just do that on a scrap of paper, of course, and that's fine if that's what you want to do. But you might find it helpful to keep all those lists and exercises—and to keep them all together. If you already keep a journal, use that. If you don't, you might want to buy one, or else just a plain spiral notebook, and keep it with this book.

Here's a real helpful suggestion: keep this book, your notebook, your Bible, and a pen or pencil together somewhere near your bed so that just before you go to sleep or just after you wake up, whichever works best for you, you can read a section of the book.

Enjoy!

Following the King into Battle

Swords clanged against shields, and battle cries rang out near the coast of what is now Scotland, on a day hundreds of years ago. A contingent of British knights, part of King Arthur's army, had been sent here to repel an invasion of Saxons, a warlike tribe from the European mainland who kept trying to conquer Britain. Arthur, meanwhile, had taken the rest of his men south to put down a rebellion there.

The men fighting in the north soon discovered that they had their hands full. The Saxons, who outnumbered them four to one, were well equipped; they had already been on British soil long enough to steal plenty of food and supplies from the British peasants.

Day after day the British met the Saxons on the battlefield, and day after day they suffered more losses and were beaten back further. One night, after two weeks of battle, when the day's fighting had stopped because it had become too dark to see, Arthur's soldiers found themselves camped along the banks of a wide, swift river. They knew that in the morning, the Saxons would attack one more time, and that this would be the end. The British had already lost most of their men and horses and weapons. The Saxons would push them back into the river, where they would either be killed by the enemy or swept away and drowned in their own heavy armor.

As they waited through the long night, they knew that they would die in the morning. They had failed their country and they had failed their king.

Then a rumor started through the camp:

"Arthur has come!"

"Arthur is here!"

And the men looked up from the cold, rocky ground where they lay trying to sleep, and there he was—their king, tall and strong, striding through the camp.

He had brought only a few men with him, but as he knelt beside each man in the camp that night, placing his hand on their shoulder and thanking them for fighting so hard against impossible odds, they felt their strength and confidence returning.

He called them together around the fire. "Tomorrow, men," he said, "we will fight together. Let us see whether these Saxon invaders fight so bravely when they face knights who are fighting beside their king!"

Next morning, the Saxons expected the British to wait along the riverbank for the attack. So they were surprised when before the sun even broke into view and before they were ready to fight, they heard British battle horns sound the charge. They looked up from their breakfast to see the British, led by King Arthur, sweeping across the fields to attack.

Even though the Saxons had ten men to every British soldier, they could not hold the battle lines against the British, who fought as they had never fought before. Pursued by Arthur and his knights, the Saxons fled back to their ships and sailed away.

What does King Arthur have to do with us today? Just this: Most of us, at least part of the time, feel like that army in the far-off north, fighting against impossible odds and with our king far away. We feel as if we're losing; we feel discouraged, hopeless. But we can't afford to sit around feeling sorry for ourselves, because there's a great battle, an important battle, going on, and we each have an important role to play in it.

We can't afford to lose. Too much is at stake.

But winning seems impossible.

We need our king to show up, put his hand on our shoulder, and say, "You're doing a great job. Nobody could have done it better. But I'm here now, and we're *really* going to fight!"

What the two of us, Ross and Dave, would like to do in this book is to show you that the King *is* here and that he'd like to help us through our feelings of discouragement and hopelessness so that we can "conquer the invaders"—fulfill the important role that God has set out for each of us to play in the cosmic drama that's unfolding all around us.

What we're involved in is better than any King Arthur legend—it's a real struggle between good and evil. God's plan for each of our lives is a blueprint for how we're to fight that battle. Each one of us is a potential hero.

But like those tired British soldiers backed up against the river, we need hope, we need encouragement. That's why we've divided this book into three sections. When you've found the encouragement and hope we've tried to provide in the first two sections, you'll be ready to accept the challenge in the third!

Verse of the Day:

Who shall separate us from the love of Christ? Shall trouble or hardship or persecution or famine or nakedness or danger or sword?. . . No, in all these things we are more than conquerors through him who loved us.

ROMANS 8:35, 37

Want to know More?

When Paul, who wrote the book of Romans, from which today's verse was taken, wrote about hardship and persecution and danger, he knew what he was talking about. Read about some of the rest of his troubles, in 2 Corinthians 11:24–27.

Just Do It:

If while those tired and disheartened soldiers were trying to sleep on that last night beside the river, one of them had turned to another and said, "You're doing a good job. Things will turn out

OK. Cheer up," the second one would have said, "Nice try. I appreciate it. But that doesn't change anything."

But when the king himself showed up and said that, it made all the difference in the world.

It was the presence of the king, not cheerful words, that saved the day.

Or to put it another way, it wasn't the words that were spoken but rather who spoke them that counted.

What we will be trying to do in this book is to turn your attention—as well as our own—back to the only one capable of curing our hopelessness and discouragement and turning us into lean, mean fighting machines!

There's an old song we used to sing in church:

Turn your eyes upon Jesus,
Look full in his wonderful face,
And the things of earth will grow strangely dim
In the light of his glory and grace.

We're hoping that in the course of using this book, your eyes will be turned toward Jesus, and all of the cares and fears of this world will grow strangely dim.

There's something that might help you to do that. Sometimes we need visual reminders; that's why we write notes to ourselves. Today find some kind of visual reminder of Jesus that you can put in your room, if you don't already have one. Maybe one of those little pictures of Jesus (as long as you remember that no one really knows what he looks like and that this is just an artist's idea), or a cross, or a poster with his name on it—something like that.

Then put it in your room, somewhere where you'll be sure to see it every morning before you leave.

That way, you can start the day aware of who your king is and of the tough battle he wants you to fight!

PART ONE

You're not as BAD OFF As you Think!

GOD LOVES YOU JUST AS YOU ARE

Forget Buddha

Dave

A friend of mine was in Bangkok not long ago. (Story of my life—my friends get to go to Bangkok and Paris, while I go to the gas station and Piggly Wiggly.) He decided to take a guided tour of the city, and one of the stops on the tour was a Buddhist temple.

You've probably never been to a Buddhist temple. I was in one in San Francisco once, and the main thing I remember is Buddhist priests running around in the hallway, banging gongs to scare the evil spirits away. And there were little golden statues of Buddha here and there. But in the Far East, they have *huge* golden statues of Buddha in the temples.

My friend Chuck watched as, one after another, the people coming into the temple brought in some small gift—maybe a couple of eggs or a flower or a chicken or a few coins—and knelt to lay that gift on the steps leading up to that huge statue. Then the visitors would bow their heads to the floor, pray, and leave.

"What's the point of the gifts?" Chuck asked his tour guide. "These people don't look as if they can afford to give anything at all, not even a couple of eggs." In Bangkok, people are either real rich or real poor—and there aren't very many rich people.

The tour guide explained, "These devout people bring these gifts, as much as they can afford, hoping that they will please the gods. In this way, they hope to find favor with the gods so that their lives will be blessed and they will avoid tragedy."

Chuck couldn't get those people out of his mind as he continued his tour of the city—or for a long time afterward. *What an amazing difference there is between what those people believe and what the Bible teaches us about God's feelings for us,* Chuck realized. *We don't have to bring gifts to God to win his favor. In fact, the Bible teaches us that he loved us and even sent his Son to die for us, before we'd done anything to deserve it at all!*

And Chuck was right. Good thing, too. Because the truth is, if we had to do something to win God's favor, we'd be out of luck. Nothing we could do would be good enough. But we don't have to.

Did you ever sing that old song:

I love him.
I love him.
Because he first loved me.
And purchased my salvation on Calvary's tree.

It's true. The Bible even says, in 1 John 4:19, "We love because he first loved us."

Don't expect Buddha to make the first move. But *our* God did, when he sent Jesus to die on the cross for us. We don't have to live in fear of what God might do to us because of his anger; what he offers us instead is his love. And what he wants to give us, because of his love, is everything good. His blessing.

We don't have to *buy* God's favor with our gifts. We already have it.

All we have to do is accept it.

Verse of the Day:

God demonstrates his own love for us in this: While we were still sinners, Christ died for us.

ROMANS 5:8

Therefore, there is now no condemnation for those who are in Christ Jesus.

ROMANS 8:1

Want to know More?

Why not read the whole passage that today's first verse comes from? It'll make you feel great about how God feels about you! Read Romans 5:1–10.

Just Do It:

What we're talking about today may be the hardest thing to understand about Christianity, even though it's so simple.

You'll notice that today I gave you two verses instead of just one. That's because they go together. Christ died for us while we were yet sinners, without our doing anything to deserve it. Therefore God loves us just as we are and doesn't condemn us for anything that we've done—or that we may yet do.

In other words, we are totally secure in his love. We know—every day when we wake up, regardless of what we did the day before—that God loves us and doesn't condemn us. We know that because the Bible tells us so.

Write those two verses on a little card and then stick it in your purse or wallet. Today take it out a few times and look at it, just to remind yourself—especially if you're feeling pretty lousy about something. Then just keep that card in there. Tomorrow or the next day, you may need a reminder.

Smile.

God loves you.

Injustice

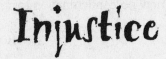

Dave

There are few things we remember longer and more vividly than the injustices done to us.

When I was in first grade, I went to a great big old school that had originally been built as a city hall. It had huge, wide hallways and an immense auditorium that had been made into a cafeteria; I had a hot lunch there every day with the rest of the students.

Schools were run differently then. More like boot camp. In fact, I think they recruited their teachers out of the Marine Corps—even the women. Before we could leave the table at lunch, we had to raise our hands and have one of the lunchroom monitors (teachers who patrolled the tables while we ate, tapping their tall black boots with their nightsticks as they sauntered past—at least, that's how I remember it) examine our plates to make sure we'd eaten everything. It didn't take us long to notice that although those monitors scrutinized our plates pretty carefully, they didn't pick them up. So we'd scoop all of our spinach off onto the table and put the plate down on top of it. Clean plate. Go play.

Despite the Gestapo, noise levels in that room often exceeded the level inside the engine of the space shuttle. We couldn't leave till our plate was clean, but as long as the monitor wasn't standing right behind us, we could shout.

Our principal, a gray-haired woman whose previous job had been as a prison guard at Alcatraz, marched up onto the stage one noon to try to quell the noise. "Attention, please!" she shouted into the squeaking mike. I could hear the heels of the monitors' black boots clicking together. "There's something you can do for me!"

And I knew what it was. "Yeah!" I shouted, trying to be helpful. I turned away from her, stood, and pointed out over the still-noisy crowd. "Shut up!" OK, it was a smart-aleck thing to do, but at least it was in character: I *was* a smart aleck.

She finished what she had to say and left the stage. I turned back to my creamed Brussels sprouts on toast. Suddenly something grabbed me by my neck and pulled me out of my chair. "You told me to shut up," my gray-haired old principal whispered in my ear.

My blood froze, but my faith in justice reassured me. This was a simple misunderstanding. All I had to do was explain what had really happened, and everything would be OK. "No," I said, "what really happened was—"

Her grip tightened. "You told me to *shut up!*" she hissed. "Me!" She dragged me down the aisle. At least I didn't have to finish my Brussels sprouts.

"Actually," I said, "I was telling *them* to shut up. All the kids. I was talking—"

"Stop lying!" she said. "We'll settle this in my office."

I didn't *want* to settle it in her office; she had a paddle in there for settling things. So I pleaded my case all the way down that huge, wide hallway, to no avail. She wasn't interested.

This was amazing! I was telling the truth and no one was interested. In my family, people got a chance to explain. Why wouldn't she listen?

And as the paddle fell on my skinny little butt, over and over again, my tears were more from outrage than pain. It was a mistake! I was being paddled for something I hadn't done!

I went back to my classroom in humiliation and sat gritting my teeth the rest of the day, without hearing a thing the teacher was saying. And I remember thinking—even as a first-grader—as I walked home past the weedy vacant lot, clenching my fists, *I wish God would grab her and tell her the truth! She didn't believe me, but she'd have to believe him!*

Yes, she would. And she will.

We live in a world of injustice. That spanking I received was the least of it. It looks pretty pale next to the injustice experienced by many families when one parent betrays his or her marriage vows to pursue an affair with another person and then divorces the spouse and abandons the children, all of whom suffer through no fault of their own. And even that is no match for the injustice experienced in many parts of the world, where people are jailed for life or even killed, sometimes for no reason at all, simply at the whim of someone in power.

But God is just. And one day, when time is over and we all kneel before God's throne, the accounts will be settled. It won't be a time for our own vengeance; we'll be too worried about the spinach that will be revealed when God, unlike the lunchroom monitors, lifts our plate. But those who have behaved unjustly will have to listen at last to the truth and then receive from God's own hands either forgiveness for their injustices or a fit punishment.

The God we serve is the hope of the downtrodden and oppressed. And he is the righteous judge of the powerful, the haughty, and the unjust.

In this life, murderers often get off scot-free, criminals don't even get arrested, employees who're doing a fine job get fired, and the people in power, like my gray-haired old prison-guard principal, inflict pain and punishment and humiliation where none is deserved.

But in the end . . .

In the end, the good guys win.

Verse of the Day:

Do not be deceived: God cannot be mocked. A man reaps what he sows.

GALATIANS 6:7

Want to know More?

See what these verses tell you about God making sure that everybody has to account for how they've behaved, whether good or bad: 1 Corinthians 4:1–5; 2 Corinthians 5:10.

Just Do It:

Take a piece of paper—*not* your journal!—and list all of the injustices that have been done to you that you can think of. Times a parent or teacher assumed you were guilty when you weren't; times a friend double-crossed you, or a boyfriend or girlfriend went out with someone else behind your back; times you didn't get the grade on your schoolwork that you should have, because of some misunderstanding; times someone should have stood up for you but didn't—and on and on.

Now read back over that list and remember all of the mental anguish that the experiences on that list have caused for you—the nights you lay awake, angry and hurt; the punishments you received that you should not have. OK, here's the sad truth: most of those experiences will not be set right by you. There is nothing you can do about them.

But there is someone who can. Put the list in front of you and pray about each of the things on it, turning them over to God to do with as he sees fit—to set right if he chooses or to ignore if he chooses. You can trust his judgment.

It might be hard for you to let go of the bitterness brought about in your life by those events—but now, if you choose to, you can. The one righteous judge has those things on his docket. He'll choose how they're to be handled. If things have to be set right, they will be one day.

So crumple that list up and throw it in the trash. You don't need it anymore.

My Army's Bigger Than Your Army

Dave

Here's one of the least-known Bible stories around, but one of the most important.

You'll find it way back in 2 Kings 6:8–23. Elisha the prophet and his servant were living in the town of Dothan. The king of Aram kept sending his army on raids to steal things from the Israelites, but God would always tell Elisha ahead of time where the raids were going to be, and Elisha would tell the king of Israel. (Talk about military intelligence!)

So each time the Arameans showed up to conduct a raid, they found the Israelite army waiting for them. Ooops!

As you would imagine, the king of Aram got ticked off after a while, so he asked his men what was going on. When he found out that the Israelites were being tipped off by a prophet, he said, "No problem. Go find out where he is and capture him." (I have a question: Under the circumstances, didn't it occur to the Arameans that Elisha would *know* they were coming? Duh!)

So the Aramean army found out that Elisha was in Dothan, and they crept in at night and surrounded the city.

Here comes the good part.

Elisha's servant got up early the next morning and went outside. (The Bible doesn't say why. Use your imagination.) Yikes! There was a huge army surrounding the city! (The Bible also doesn't say how far along he'd got with what he'd gone out there to do, before he realized all those eyes were watching him. Could have been embarrassing.)

He called Elisha outside, and as the two of them stood looking at the vast army of the enemy surrounding them, the servant whimpered, "Oh, my lord, what shall we do?"

"Don't be afraid," Elisha answered him. "Those who are with us are more than those who are with them." Now, if that seems like kind of a weird answer to you, imagine how it seemed to the servant. The two of them were standing there alone, facing an army!

But then Elisha prayed, "O Lord, open his eyes so he may see." And the Lord *did* open that servant's eyes, and suddenly he saw reality a lot differently. Because behind the army of the Arameans, he could see another army. The hills, in fact, were full of soldiers and horses and chariots—all of them burning with fire! God's army! And it was a whole lot bigger than the army of the Arameans.

What an amazing thing! The story goes on, of course: God caused the Arameans to go blind, and then Elisha offered to lead them to where they wanted to go. When God gave the Arameans back their sight, they discovered that Elisha had led them right to the king of Israel and his army! The Israelites, being in a good mood, fed the Arameans and sent them home to their king, who wisely decided to stop the raids.

But the part I like best is right where God opens the servant's eyes and he sees that no matter how hopeless things look to him, God's still got everything under control—that God's army is a lot bigger than the bad guys' army. Why do I like that part? Because I'm like that servant. Most of the time, I'm worried that I'm about one step away from disaster—that I'm surrounded by bad guys who are just about to do me in.

Are you like that, too? Probably so; most of us are. We look at the "armies" surrounding us—friends or family who seem to be rejecting us, feelings of depression or anger, temptations we give in to again and again, tasks like schoolwork that just seem beyond our ability—and we say, like Elisha's servant, "Oh, my lord, what shall we do?"

Maybe we need God to open our eyes so we can see that *his* army is bigger than *their* army.

Verse of the Day:

"Don't be afraid. . . . Those who are with us are more than those who are with them." And Elisha prayed, "O Lord, open his eyes so he may see." Then the Lord opened the servant's eyes, and he looked and saw the hills full of horses and chariots of fire all around Elisha.

2 KINGS 6:16–17

Want to know More?

Read the whole story: 2 Kings 6:8–23.

Just Do It:

Want to have your eyes opened like the servant's eyes were? Then, pray a prayer something like Elisha prayed, only pray it for yourself: "Lord, sometimes my faith is weak. Sometimes I can't really sense you or your angels around me, protecting me. Help me to see that, Lord; open my eyes, like Elisha's servant, so that I can see how mighty you are and how puny my fears are next to your strength."

I believe that God will honor that prayer. He may not make you see chariots of fire on the hills all around you. But he will strengthen your faith to believe in what you can't see.

Tom

Dave

"Hey, guys!" Tom would yell as he and I stepped out of my car in the high school parking lot. "How's it goin', you warthogs?" And he would wave his huge bag of cheap cookies in the air.

"Hey, it's Tom!" "All right!" "Gimme a cookie!" the crowd of guys would yell back, and Tom would be immediately surrounded by teenage boys reaching past each other to get a hand in his bag of goodies.

Tom Murphy was one of those guys no one ever forgets. He was big, probably six feet four inches, and solid—he'd gone to college on a football scholarship. He was also loud, and just crude enough to make some adults uneasy. And he always seemed happy. No, not just happy—ecstatic, joyful, unable to keep from laughing. Except when he was upset about something, of course, in which case he was absolutely miserable, positive that his life was ruined. Five minutes later he'd be ecstatic again. And he was a committed Christian.

Tom had volunteered to be a leader in the Young Life group I was heading up. I quickly discovered that one of Tom's strengths was that high school students loved him. This trip to our local high school campus was just like all the others: Tom spent the entire trip surrounded by students, both guys and girls, who wanted one of his cookies. But it wasn't really the cookies; they just liked being around Tom.

And as usual, this time I trailed along behind, greeting the few students I knew by name.

"Hey, Chip. How's it goin'? Andy, hey. Gonna be at Young Life tonight?"

And they would nod a quick greeting my way as they hurried on to join the huge group surrounding Tom.

OK, I admit it. Sometimes I felt a little twinge of jealousy that Tom, who had just come onto the scene where I'd been active for years, should have immediately become so much more popular with the students than I was. But only a little twinge and only sometimes, because I very much valued Tom and the contribution he made to our Young Life team. He had gifts that I, obviously, didn't have. But that was OK. God had given him those gifts, and who was I to argue with God?

Besides, the rest of us on the staff had gifts of our own:

- I recruited the staff, trained them, and conducted all of our staff meetings and Bible studies—things that Tom could never have done. Those just weren't his gifts.
- Mark was a great song leader and good at taking students on outdoor adventures—skiing, camping, canoeing. Both Tom and Mark were single, which gave them more uncommitted time to spend with our Young Life group, whereas I was married with kids and had demands on my time.
- Melissa's personality made her something of a female Tom, and she had a great sense of humor; the high school girls all loved her.
- Warren, her husband, was quieter, but he had a good-paying job that allowed him to underwrite the expense of a lot of our Young Life activities, and his compassion and personal spiritual commitment helped the rest of us keep our priorities straight.

I could go on, but I think the point is clear. God brought a group of us together from different backgrounds, each with different gifts, to do a job he wanted done. No one person could have done that job—but the whole team of us, with our wide variety of personalities and gifts and talents, could handle it.

Working together, we made a difference in the lives of a lot of high school students in that town, for many years.

It's fair to say that anyone who had come to us and said, "I really love what you're doing with Young Life and I'd like to help, but I don't know what I could do—I'm not really good at anything," would have found a useful role on our staff. Because despite what we may think, *everybody* is good at something. God promises us that.

In fact, the Bible talks about all Christians as being the *body* of Christ. Each of us is some part of that body. And God makes it real clear, too, that there's no part of the body that's worth more than any other part:

> But God has combined the members of the body and has given greater honor to the parts that lacked it, so that there should be no division in the body, but that its parts should have equal concern for each other. If one part suffers, every part suffers with it; if one part is honored, every part rejoices with it.

1 CORINTHIANS 12:24–26

Sadly, I have known many people, both teenagers and adults, who have truly believed that they had nothing to offer to God, to offer to the church, to offer to anyone—that they had no gifts, no talents, no attractive thing about them that anyone would appreciate.

Is God a liar? No, of course not. So since the Bible clearly tells us that he gave each of us gifts that he wants us to use on his behalf, you have those gifts, just as I do.

We all have gifts. The only question is: Are we willing to use them?

Verse of the Day:

> Now you are the body of Christ, and each one of you is a part of it.

1 CORINTHIANS 12:27

Want to know More?

Read the entire passage from which today's verse is taken: 1 Corinthians 12:12–27. And remember—God made you a part of that body, too.

Just Do It:

I'm not going to ask you to complete a "gifts analysis" to determine all of the abilities and talents that God has given you, and set out a ten-year plan for how you're going to develop them. (That's tomorrow's activity—no, just kidding.)

Instead, I want to encourage you to do something very simple today. Just think of one thing that you do well. Just one. Are you good at encouraging and building up other people? Praying? Challenging people who are about to act wrongly, persuading them not to make that mistake? Being a friend? Making new friends? Sharing the good news about Jesus Christ with people? Inviting people to church? Helping people solve their problems? Giving people rides in your car? Helping them with their homework?

Just think of one thing you do well—and today do it for someone. Do it to help them. Do it in a way that you think will please God.

Sound simple? It is. But it's an important step on the way to taking your place in the body of Christ.

Just Wait, Chrissie

Dave

I've always wondered what happened to Chrissie.

She was in the Young Life group Tom and I worked with. Some weeks, between Bible study and all of the craft projects that she and the other girls had started and kept dropping by to work on, she was in my home about every night. Which was OK with my family—Chrissie was an easy girl to like.

Chrissie loved to laugh, she loved the outdoors, she loved the Lord, she loved music, she loved her friends—sometimes it seemed as if she loved everyone and everything.

Except herself.

Chrissie had a problem common among teenagers. She couldn't find anything she really liked about herself. She didn't like her looks—too boyish. She didn't like her sense of humor; everyone else did, but later, looking back, she always felt that she'd made a fool of herself. Sometimes it seemed as if Chrissie's favorite activity was sitting around worrying about something she'd done the day before and how it must have looked to everyone, how immature she'd been, how badly she'd hurt someone's feelings, and so on.

"I'm just no good," she would wail. "I'll never amount to anything! People should just give up on me! Why am I even a Christian? I don't deserve anybody's love, let alone God's! What good am I ever going to do him? He can't use a piece of garbage like me!"

At times like that, I would try to get Chrissie to hear a couple of very important things, but I don't think she ever heard me.

The first thing was this: *Nobody's perfect.*

We compare ourselves with others: John's a better athlete than I am; Jenny's so much prettier; Alice is a brain and I'm a dipstick; Dirk's so tall and I'm so short; Freida can always think of just the right thing to say while I stand around saying, "Duh . . ."

What we don't think of during those comparisons is that each of those people also has things they hate about themselves and that they play the same game. Sure, John's a good athlete. But he hates his acne and his high voice and his grades. Sure, Jenny's pretty, but she thinks her thighs are too fat and her legs are too short, and what she'd really like to be able to do is play the piano like you. Freida's a good conversationalist, but she hates her looks and she's always in the doctor's office for her asthma.

Nobody's perfect. We all have our good points and our bad points. And God was the one who gave us that set of characteristics, so we can be sure that there's some pretty good stuff in there, even if we haven't found it yet.

The second thing was this: *God isn't finished with us yet.*

The truth is, we don't just become mature, wise, well-adjusted people overnight. It takes a long time—a lifetime, in fact. Chrissie blamed herself for acting immaturely. But how did she expect herself to act? She *was* immature! And you don't simply become mature on your sixteenth—or nineteenth or twenty-first—birthday. Or your fortieth, for that matter. Nor do you mature in all areas at once. Our bodies begin to mature sexually at puberty, for instance, but our emotions and our judgment lag far behind.

Think of maturity as a verb, not a noun. It's a *process,* and that process is called "learning from your mistakes." So instead of kicking yourself for the dumb things you've done, learn to think of them as a necessary part of becoming the person you want to be.

Over and over, I would say to Chrissie in as many different ways as I knew how, "Be patient with yourself, girl. Give yourself a break. Not even God expects you to be as good as you expect yourself to be."

Did Chrissie hear that message? I don't know; after she graduated from high school and went off to college, we lost contact. But if she did, I'm sure that the next several years went much smoother for her.

As they will for you.

Verse of the Day:

. . . being confident of this, that he who began a good work in you will carry it on to completion until the day of Christ Jesus.

PHILIPPIANS 1:6

Want to know More?

That's a great book, Philippians—one of my favorites. And here's another passage, which tells us that even the guy who wrote Philippians, Paul, wasn't as mature and godly as he wanted to be, and expected to keep getting better and wiser: Philippians 3:12–15.

Just Do It:

This is where you could really use the perspective of an adult friend—a parent, if you can talk easily and openly with your parents, or a youth worker or school counselor. Today ask for a few minutes to talk with that adult about some things that are troubling you. Share with him or her the things that bother you the most about yourself or that you worry about the most. Ask for some help in putting those things into perspective.

Maybe what that person says will sound as trite as some of the slogans I quoted above: *Nobody's perfect. God isn't finished with you yet.* But listen anyway. There's a great deal of truth behind those clichés.

Whatever Happened to the Class of . . .

Ross

When you think "homecoming," you probably think of a home football game that you really hope your team wins, the crowning of a homecoming king and queen, a homecoming dance . . .

But believe it or not, students aren't the only ones who have special activities at homecoming. Why do they call it "homecoming," after all? It's the one weekend during the year when alumni—those who once attended that school but have already graduated, even if their graduation was fifty years ago—are encouraged to return to their alma mater to see the old school, remind themselves of their own high school days, and meet their old classmates again.

I love homecoming! I try to go to as many of them at Highland High School as I can. It's really neat to see how everyone has changed. Of course, there's a lot of mental comparing that goes on: Am I aging as much as Phil is? Is Donna still more beautiful than anyone else? Does Andy still look like the jock he used to be? How do I stack up careerwise against the rest of the graduates?

Those mental comparisons are pretty interesting. One thing you might expect, for instance, is that the people who were the most popular and successful back when they were in high school—the best athletes, the student body presidents, the homecoming queens—would have become the most successful adults. Right? I mean, after all, they had the confidence, the ability . . .

Wrong. By the time we'd been out of high school for ten years, most of the campus big shots were falling so far short of their own expectations, as well as everyone else's, that they stopped showing up for homecoming at all. It was too embarrassing for them.

So who were the high schoolers who became the most successful adults? You guessed it. Not the ones who'd had it made at seventeen, driving daddy's new sports car, scoring the game-winning touchdown, winning every election or honor. No, the ones who became the most successful adults were the ones who'd struggled through high school: the wallflowers, the ones who'd often felt unpopular, unaccepted, out of place, who'd not been able to catch a pass in gym class, much less in a real football game, who'd had too much acne to have a shot at homecoming anything, who'd been too fat or too skinny, who'd never won an election or honor of any kind, except maybe in band or in academics—two areas that never seemed to guarantee popularity in my high school.

I'm proud of my old gang of "misfits." Take Preston Jones—a real low-key guy who'd just drifted along at Highland. He hadn't been popular. But he became one of America's outstanding playwrights, writing a tremendously popular group of plays called *A Texas Trilogy*.

One of my high school best friends was Jimmy Stringer, who became a movie director.

Another friend, Joe Patterson, became the chief of the navy's engineering unit—a huge responsibility.

I could give a lot more examples, but the point is this: Honor and glory and popularity in high school—the things all high school students want—don't really prepare you to face real life. But facing the ordinary, everyday problems of high school life *does* prepare you to face the ordinary, everyday struggles, disappointments, and failures of life in the real world. Your teenage years are full of pressure and struggle. Surprise, surprise. So is the rest of life. Learning to face and overcome those struggles and disappointments at seventeen gives you, in adult life, a boost over those who breezed through high school in a cloud of glory—and therefore will have to learn to deal with disappointments at twenty-five.

If this sounds like a backdoor way of getting you to see the difficulties in your life in a more positive way, then I guess that's exactly what it is. Steelworkers harden steel, making it tough so that it will last in use, by repeatedly heating it red-hot and then plunging it into cold water. That wouldn't feel very good to me if I were a piece of steel. Nor do the difficulties of life—the embarrassments, the disappointments, the failures, the griefs—feel very good to us. But those are the things that make us tough, that give us the strength to endure.

Those are the things that teach us to depend on ourselves, that teach us that there won't always be someone, a parent or some other helper, waiting in the wings to ride in and rescue us.

Those are the things that teach us to trust God to help us.

Verse of the Day:

"For I know the plans I have for you," declares the LORD, "plans to prosper you and not to harm you, plans to give you hope and a future."

JEREMIAH 29:11

Want to know More?

Read Psalm 40. Doesn't this sound like something you might say when you realize how, even in the hard parts of your life, God is working for your good?

Just Do It:

Make a quick mental list: What are the things that bother you the most about your life right now? Your appearance? Your lack of friends? Your lack of ability in some area, such as athletics or academics or the art of making conversation? Once you've identified a half dozen things, brainstorm a little. In what ways can those disappointments be strengthening you for success later in life? Could they, for instance, be preparing you to succeed where others have failed, by giving you the ability to keep on going when things get tough?

I hope that you'll be able to see the problems and disappointments you're facing now as opportunities. And to help you face them, please memorize today's verse, Jeremiah 29:11. When you get discouraged, repeat that verse to yourself. It will help.

"Folksingers, Where Are You?"

Dave

"Hello?"

"Hello. Is this Dave Lambert?"

"Yep."

"Of Tim and Dave, the folksinger guys?"

I listened a little harder. "Yeah. It sure is."

"Good. I work with the Dave Wilkerson rallies. Mr. Wilkerson is going to be holding a rally at Melodyland next month, and we wondered if you guys would be able to sing at it."

Was he kidding? Usually, Tim and I sang for audiences of a couple of dozen kids at a church youth group or Campus Life club. But Dave Wilkerson rallies were *big*! Melodyland held about 3,500 people. And now some guy was asking *us* to play there? *Us?*

"Well," I said, playing it cool, "give me the details, and I'll talk it over with Tim, my partner. We'll try to make it if we can."

Ha. We'd have canceled *anything* to be able to play there. We thought of little else for a month, and finally the big night came. We dressed up in our favorite outfits, showed up about two hours early so we could treat ourselves to dinner at Denny's right across the street, and then, trembling with excitement, carried our guitar cases into the artists' entrance to Melodyland.

Everyone was rushing around carrying speakers or huge coils of electrical cord; no one seemed to notice us. Finally the guy who seemed to be in charge rushed past, did a double take, and stopped just long enough to tell us that we'd be on first. "We'll actually get you started while people are still walking in," he said as he grabbed someone else walking by that he needed to talk to, "so there'll be some noise. Don't worry about it; the people who're already seated will be able to hear you just fine." He pointed us to our dressing rooms. "Somebody'll come get you five minutes before show time."

That was a little disappointing; we'd envisioned 3,500 people sitting, listening attentively to us. Now it turned out that some of them would still be walking in, finding their seats . . . "Well, big deal," Tim said, shrugging it off as we settled into our dressing room—which we didn't really need, because we were already dressed. "By the time we finish, they'll all be here, anyway."

So we sat around getting nervous for a half hour or so, wondering when we'd get that knock on the door. Finally Tim said, "You know, there's something funny."

"What's that?" I asked.

"Well," he answered, "I wonder why they didn't ask us to sing through the mikes for a minute or two, so they could get a volume level—"

And then we heard it, booming through the loudspeakers—and I don't mean just through the speakers in our room, I mean throughout the whole huge auditorium: "FOLKSINGERS, WHERE ARE YOU?"

We looked at each other. "Us?" I asked.

We grabbed our guitars and ran down the hallway to the auditorium. It was about half full already. Somebody we'd never seen before, who was wearing a pair of headphones, grabbed us. "You guys are supposed to be up there! Go on! Move!"

"Don't you want to get a level on the mikes?" I asked.

"Too late!" He gestured us toward the stage. "Go! Sing!"

We trotted up onto the stage, and there was a smattering of applause. We stepped up to our mikes and launched into our first song.

SKREEK!

Feedback screamed from the huge speakers; the volume was turned up way too high. Then the engineer must have cut it back to almost nothing; we could barely hear ourselves. We looked at each other, frantic, but kept singing.

There was a little bit of polite applause after our first song, probably from our parents and friends and people who felt sorry for us. But we couldn't hear it, because the rest of the crowd was being so noisy. Church youth groups, feeling hyper, started some church-spirit yells: "We're from First Baptist, how 'bout you . . ."

We started our second song. We were halfway through it before we realized that mine was the only voice coming through. On our third song, only the guitar mikes were on; there were no voices at all. And we looked at each other with a glum realization: they were using us to *test* the mikes, turning each one off and on, higher and lower, adjusting tone and volume—so that when the *real* musicians got onstage, everything would be just right.

We were just the guinea pigs. Our music was expendable.

And in front of a couple thousand people, no less, including our parents and girlfriends.

Mercifully, our fifteen minutes ended. We bowed, smiled, and walked offstage, back to our dressing room. We put our guitars away and looked at each other, but all we could do was shake our heads.

After the show, Tim's brother Jay found us. "Well?" I asked.

He just shook his head. "You don't want to know."

"Come on," Tim said. "I mean, we couldn't have sounded *that* bad. Could we?"

"You really don't want to know," Jay said.

It's been almost thirty years since that night, and finally I can admit it: we sounded lousy. And really, we knew it when we slumped back to our car that night and drove away. We felt humiliated. We felt worse than useless. And we knew beyond a shadow of a doubt what we had already suspected: there was no future for us in music; we ought to just sell our guitars and go to work at a gas station.

We survived, obviously. Life, after all, is a learning process, and many of its lessons are painful—but few are fatal. I wish Tim and I could have remembered, as we scrambled, nervous and alarmed, onto the stage that night, that we weren't going through anything Jesus hadn't already gone through before us—a thousand times worse, in fact. Remember Palm Sunday? He rode into Jerusalem on a donkey, and the people gathered along the roadside to spread palm branches on the road in front of him—symbolizing royalty—and to shout, "Hosanna!"

A week later the same crowd was yelling, "Crucify him! Crucify him!"

Jesus too had the experience of moving from the peak to the pit in short order. I'm sure he had no difficulty understanding how we felt—or for that matter, how *you* feel when the things you expect to become your greatest triumphs become your most bitter failures.

He's been there.

Verse of the Day:

For we do not have a high priest who is unable to sympathize with our weaknesses, but we have one who has been tempted in every way, just as we are—yet was without sin. Let us then approach the throne of grace with confidence, so that we may receive mercy and find grace to help us in our time of need.

HEBREWS 4:15–16

Want to know More?

Here's a passage that'll help us learn to put our weaknesses into perspective: 2 Corinthians 12:9–10.

Just Do It:

Despite our painful discouragement that night, Tim and I kept at it, kept trying to get better. I decided eventually that my best talents were as a writer—of songs, yes, but also of stories. Tim decided that his best talents lay in managing the musical careers of others. We pursued those areas.

For the past couple of years, Tim has produced the Grammy Awards show.

Many of my songs were published, and I eventually recorded an album. But I found greater success with my stories and articles, and now it's safe to say that millions of people have read my magazine articles or one or more of the six books I've written.

Do I tell you this to brag about our success? No. I tell you this because there have been times when you've felt as bad about yourself as Tim and I felt that night, when you've felt that you were hopeless, that you'd wasted your big chances, that you were doomed to be a failure, washed up before you were twenty years old.

The success you'll be later on in life will be built upon those failures and upon the lessons you learned from them.

What did Tim and I learn that night? For one thing, we learned that there's no such thing as only one chance. God gives us many chances. If we blow one, we'll get another—and we'll be better able to excel at the second one (or the third one or the fourth one), because of what we learned from our mistakes the first time around.

Another thing we *could* have learned that night—but didn't learn, unfortunately, until many years later—was to take advantage of the truths in today's verse. Jesus *does* know what we're feeling; he has felt all of this and more—all of the temptations we feel, all of the rejection, all of the loneliness and sense of failure and uncertainty. When we pray, then, we can be confident that he understands *exactly* what we're feeling. And sympathizes with us.

Yesterday you listed the things that bother you most about yourself—your disappointments, failures, rejections. Read today's verse again and then calmly and confidently pray about those failures—list them for God, remind him of how miserable you felt for weeks afterward, how disappointed you were, how you cried, how you wanted to die. Then ask him to take those failures and turn them into something good in your life, to reveal to you the precious lessons hidden in each one, to show you how you have been—without realizing it—strengthened and made wiser by those mistakes.

Then ask God humbly for those second chances. And when they come, don't be afraid to try again.

selling the House

Ross

I answered the knock at the door. "Hey, Mike," I said. "Come on in."

"I've only got a minute," Mike said. He'd been one of my classmates in medical school, which we'd just finished. I was in the process of selling my house and packing up to move to Charlotte, North Carolina, where I would serve my internship at Charlotte Memorial Hospital. Mike was staying in Florida; he would intern at a local hospital.

The medical school years had been hard for my wife, Pat, and me; we'd struggled financially, and we'd had to make the difficult decision to put our daughter Cathy into a hospital for the mentally retarded, where she could get the care she needed. I was looking forward to a new start in Charlotte—but first I had to sell this house.

And that was just what Mike had come to talk about. "This is a great place, Ross. My wife and I will need a place to live while I intern here—our apartment's just too small and old. How much do you hope to get for this place?"

I told him.

He shook his head. "Can't go that high. But a lot of that will go for Realtor's fees, right?"

"The usual percentage," I said.

"OK. So let's do it this way: fire your Realtor; then I'll pay you five percent less than you're asking. You'll get the same amount, and I'll save a few thousand bucks."

I frowned. "Doesn't really sound honest. I wouldn't be dealing in good faith with my Realtor." I shook my head. "Sorry, Mike. Make my Realtor an offer, and see what he says."

Mike grumbled and left, and I felt a bit guilty for not being able to help my classmate.

I felt better an hour later, though, when my Realtor called with an offer from someone else—someone who was willing to pay what we were asking.

Mike called the next day. "Change your mind yet?" he asked.

"No," I replied. "In fact, I accepted an offer on the house yester—"

"You *what*?" Mike exploded.

"I accepted an offer. I sold the house."

"But I talked to you *first*!" he spluttered.

"Yes, but you didn't offer what I was asking, and besides, I told you you'd have to talk to my Realtor. Did you do that?"

"Of course not!" he shouted. "That was the whole point! We could have both saved money!"

"Well, I didn't think—"

"So was this guy you sold my house to a classmate of yours? Was he?"

"No, but—"

"So it doesn't mean much to you, apparently, that we struggled through med school together—and besides," he went on, "you'll be making a whole lot more at Charlotte Memorial than I will down here. I mean, you guys'll be *rich* up there, and we'll be struggling along—still living in that same crummy apartment, for all you care. Hey—did you sign anything yet, Ross? Maybe it's not too late to call the whole thing off. You're going to feel rotten about this whole thing, Ross. Do yourself a favor. Just call your Realtor . . ."

And on and on he went. Fortunately, a couple of things were clear to me as he rambled on. For one, he was trying to control *my* behavior to accomplish *his* goals. My goal was to sell the house so that I could move to Charlotte, and I'd already accomplished that, fairly and honestly. He didn't care about that—he only cared about *his* goal: to buy my house. And second, it was obvious that the way he was trying to control, or manipulate, my behavior was through guilt—through trying to make me feel that I was a bad person or that I'd done something very wrong, so that I would do what he wanted.

Mike wasn't the first person to try to control my behavior by making me feel guilty, nor was he the last. Unfortunately, it's pretty common—not just in my life but in the lives of most people.

And it's a problem wherever it occurs, but especially for Christians. Why? Because we want to be led by the Holy Spirit. We want *God* to control our decisions and attitudes. And that can't happen if someone else—*anyone* else—is controlling us to make us do what *they* want.

How about you? Do you ever find yourself behaving in a way you don't really want to, because someone else expresses anger and criticism when you behave in the way you'd prefer? If so, you're not alone. Tomorrow I want to tell you about a girl named Claudia, who experienced the same thing. In fact, this subject is so important that we'll be talking about it for the next three days.

Verse of the Day:

As water reflects a face, so a man's heart reflects the man.

PROVERBS 27:19

Want to know More?

Check out these verses about how real friends treat each other: Job 2:11; Psalm 35:14; Proverbs 17:9; 17:17; 22:24; 27:9.

Just Do It:

"As water reflects a face, so a man's heart reflects the man," today's verse says. And often how your friends treat you when they want something from you is a good way to tell what's in their heart. Do they let you make up your own mind about what's best for you? Or do they, like Mike in this story, try to force you to do what they want, regardless of what's best for you?

Make a list. Identify a half dozen times within the past year that someone has told you something about yourself that made you feel small, bad, or guilty.

Was it a teacher who yelled at you when you did something wrong, like forgetting your homework?

A parent who got all over your case about something you said or did—or forgot to do?

A friend who made you feel that you were being selfish or disloyal when you wouldn't do what he or she wanted?

Not all of these incidents, of course, were attempts to control you by making you feel guilty. Your parent, for instance, may have just been angry and frustrated that you seemed rebellious or irresponsible. When you start to feel down on yourself because of what others say to you, it's important to be able to recognize what's going on.

Keep that list. We'll look at it again over the next couple of days.

Claudia

Ross

I walked out into the waiting room to find my next appointment. It was the first one for this client, so I didn't know her by sight. "Claudia?" I asked.

A teenage girl stood up. There were two things I noticed about her immediately. One was that she was beautiful. The other was that she looked incredibly sad. Even though she smiled and tried to seem pleasant, her eyes looked out from a place of hurt and discouragement and depression.

I glanced at her chart as I ushered her back into my office. Sixteen years old. Formerly a top student, but now losing all interest in school; withdrawing from family and friends; spending a great deal of time alone in her room, doing nothing; subject to wild mood swings and long bouts of crying.

As we talked, my initial suspicions seemed to be confirmed. Claudia was deeply depressed. And she was a very sensitive girl in many ways—including her deep sensitivity and vulnerability to the attitudes of others about herself. But like most depressed teenagers, she really wasn't aware that she was depressed or that she was so much affected by the attitudes of others. She simply thought that all those bad things people said about her were true.

"Tell me about your boyfriend," I said.

Unlike most teenagers in love, her eyes didn't light up, she didn't blush or smile shyly. When I mentioned her boyfriend, she seemed startled into a sudden fear. "Mark," she said.

"What's he like?" I asked.

"Oh, he's wonderful," she said, but her expression didn't match her words.

"You think you'll still be going together a year from now?"

She grimaced. "I'd *like* to."

"But?"

She almost whispered, "But I don't think I'll be able to hold on to him that long."

Eventually, over several visits, Claudia grew comfortable enough around me to confide that she and Mark were engaging in sexual activities that made Claudia very uncomfortable, that violated her morals. Why was she doing these things, then? Because Mark had discovered that Claudia, because she was so sensitive to the opinions of others, could be manipulated into doing things she didn't want to do.

You don't really love me.

Can't you see how I feel, Claudia? Aren't my feelings important?

You're just a tease, leading me on and then backing off. It's your fault I feel this way.

If you really cared about me, you would . . .

Mark knew how to control her. And he had used that simple technique to make her behave in ways that caused her to feel deep guilt and condemnation. And of course, his constant scolding and criticism made her feel even worse. She felt worthless in his eyes and in her own.

"You're a very sensitive girl, Claudia. Did you know that?" I said to her one day. "You're sensitive in many ways. One of them is that you're strongly affected by the things others say about you. Even if they're not true."

She looked at me, puzzled.

So I told her the story of my friend Mike and selling my house in Florida. Then I said, "Do you see how his words to me were spoken for *his* good and not for mine—how, in fact, his words were designed to hurt me by causing me to do something that I'd have felt guilty about?"

Slowly Claudia nodded, still not sure where I was heading, but beginning to see a connection.

"Claudia, when your boyfriend asks you to do something that you feel is wrong, do you see that he's using the same method Mike did with me? Do you see that he tries to make you feel guilty so that you'll do what *he* wants, rather than what you feel is right? The things he says about you simply aren't true. They're just a way to manipulate you. Let me ask you something. Would you ever make *him* do something that would be harmful to him or that would make him feel terrible?"

She looked shocked. "Of course not."

I leaned forward. "Then, Claudia—if he really cares about you, why is he making you do things that hurt you?"

I watched as she retreated into herself, searching for the truth in her relationship with Mark. And I watched as the truth slowly seeped into her understanding. A painful truth—but a freeing one as well, and the tears that came into her eyes couldn't hide the look of freedom and triumph as she realized that she didn't have to allow herself to be controlled through guilt.

The next time I saw Claudia, there was a new sparkle in her eye. Her depression was gradually lifting, and her behavior was returning to the healthy patterns of a normal teenager.

And Mark was history.

Verse of the Day:

Therefore, there is now no condemnation for those who are in Christ Jesus, because through Christ Jesus the law of the Spirit of life set me free from the law of sin and death.

ROMANS 8:1–2

Want to know More?

Read the entire eighth chapter of Romans. It's one of the most remarkable chapters in the Bible!

Just Do It:

Take another look at the list you made yesterday after reading "Selling the House." It should contain about a half dozen instances of someone saying things to you that made you feel bad about yourself in some way. Today you're going to refine that list a little bit. Read through it again, and this time identify the times that the person who made you feel bad about yourself did so in order to get you to do something you didn't want to do.

Maybe a friend called you chicken so that you would do what they wanted.

Maybe someone tried to get you to change your mind by making you feel that your original decision was going to hurt them.

Mark on your list the thing you *really* wanted to do—your goal—and the thing the other person wanted you to do—*their* goal.

How many times did you actually change your mind and do what the other person wanted, rather than what you wanted? Looking back now, which of the two options do you think would have been the best?

Keep this list. You may want to use it again tomorrow.

The "Manipulation Maneuver"

There are two kinds of people in the world: sensitive people and insensitive people.

OK, OK, that's simplifying. We're all sensitive to some degree, but some of us are a lot more sensitive than others.

The *more* sensitive people tend to be:

- sensitive to the way others around them feel, which sometimes makes them good listeners and comforting, caring people.
- careful about what they say, because they don't want to hurt anyone's feelings.
- sensitive to others' remarks about them, which sometimes makes them worry too much about what others say or think. You've probably heard people say, when they see someone burst into tears at a minor insult or "insensitive" remark, "Oh, she's being too sensitive."

And then there are the *less* sensitive people. They tend to be:

- "thick-skinned," or able to ignore the insults or criticism of others, because to be honest, they don't really care much what others think of them.
- less careful about how they treat or speak to others, because they often don't realize—or don't care—that they're hurting someone's feelings.

What kind of person was Claudia, the sixteen-year-old that Ross talked about in yesterday's reading? Right. Sensitive. What kind of person was Mark, her boyfriend (soon to be ex-boyfriend)? Right again. Insensitive.

And that's often how it works with guilt manipulation. Sensitive people are more susceptible to guilt manipulators, because they care so deeply how others feel and what others say. Tell a sensitive person that she's hurt your feelings, and she'll fall all over herself trying to make it up to you. Less sensitive people, on the other hand, are more apt to try to *use* manipulation on others, since they're less likely to care that their actions are hurting someone else.

The "manipulation maneuver" itself is very simple: the manipulator finds ways to make the manipulatee feel guilty if he or she doesn't do what the manipulator wants. Claudia's relationship with Mark was a classic example, and one that, unfortunately, is often repeated around the country. Boys whose sex drive is much stronger than their sensitivity try to pressure girls to have a sexual encounter with them, by—in a strange reversal of moral standards—making the girls feel guilty if they *don't*. "If you really loved me, you would . . ." And of course, many girls fall for it, as Claudia did, because they so badly want their boyfriend to know how much they love him.

But that's only one instance of guilt manipulation. It shows up in every area of our lives, not just in sexual ways. The truth is, if you can be manipulated by others through guilt or intimidation, you will *always* be in danger of being controlled by others, in *every* area of your life. You'll have goals of your own—but you'll be in danger of not realizing those goals, because someone else will always be able to turn you in the direction of *their* goals instead.

How do you combat it? How do you arm yourself against those who would try to control you through guilt? We'll talk about that below, after we look at today's verses—verses that remind us that as Christians, we have a special reason to resist control by others. Often, obeying God means making decisions that won't be popular with the people around us, especially if those people aren't living for God themselves. If we're to obey God, we need to be able to resist the attempts of those people to control us.

And God will help you to do just that.

Verse of the Day:

"We must obey God rather than men!"

ACTS 5:29

Want to know More?

Read that entire fifth chapter of Acts. It's a great example of how Peter and the rest of the disciples were able to resist the efforts of others who tried to control them by claiming that wrong was right.

Just Do It:

This whole section on guilt manipulation may seem like a foreign language to some of you. *I don't do this, and I don't see anybody doing it to me,* you might be thinking. *Why is this book spending so much time on it?*

If that's you, then just file this information away. It may come in handy later when you run into a real guilt manipulator.

But if you've seen yourself in these stories about guilt manipulation, then maybe some mental exercises will help you bring that situation under control.

First, *identify the people in your life who try to control you by making you feel guilty or who try to confuse you so that you'll think wrong is right.* You'll probably find some of them on that list you've been using for the past couple of days.

Second, *identify the areas of conflict in your life right now.* Is someone trying to get you to change a decision through guilt manipulation? Is someone trying to get you to change the way you behave? List those current conflicts. Some of them you may have been struggling with for a long time—and again, you might find them on your list.

Third, *figure out a way to claim your right to make your own decisions*. It might be as simple as just telling someone to back off. Or you might have to set up a session with that person and a counselor so that you can have the opportunity to speak your mind without fearing that the manipulative person will emotionally overpower you.

Remember: it's often hard for people who are being manipulated to openly resist the people who are controlling them. That's because manipulatees are *sensitive* people, right? And sensitive people are often afraid of hurting others' feelings.

Maybe that's why a normal and justifiable reaction to someone who tries to control you through guilt is *anger*. And that anger is not only normal, it's also useful. It can help you—especially if you're one of those sensitive people who don't like to hurt someone's feelings—to get past that hurdle and say, "Hey! Knock it off. You're trying to make me do something that I don't feel good about, and I don't appreciate it. I don't try to control what you do, and I'd like you to let me make my own decisions, too, all right? And this one's already made, so let's not hear any more about it."

Those aren't easy words for a sensitive person to speak. We need God's help to find that boldness. So the fourth step is: *pray*. Before you actually take the course of action you've just chosen, spend some time in prayer. And the God who wants you to behave in a way that honors him will strengthen you as you try to regain control of your own life!

"You're a Lousy Speaker!"

Dave

Remember my musical partner, Tim? You read, in "Folksingers, Where Are You?" about our disaster at Melodyland. We made a good musical team, Tim and I. Tim didn't write music and wasn't as good on guitar, but he had a better business head and was good at getting bookings. Our talents complemented each other.

Even so, not long after the Melodyland experience, some significant conflicts began to develop between us. Tim, it became clear, wanted to be "the leader."

Now, I could see why a larger musical group would need a leader. But why would two guys singing together need a leader? You just talk things over and decide what to do! So after Tim had introduced himself to our audiences a couple of times as "the leader" of Tim and Dave, I decided we'd better have a talk.

It didn't go well. Tim insisted that a group of any size needed a leader, someone to make the call when the members can't come to agreement, someone to represent the rest in negotiations, and so on.

"Look—let's just split up the responsibilities, then," I said. "By ability. You're good at the business end, so you handle bookings, finances, et cetera. You call the shots there. I'm better at the musical end, so I'll decide on arrangements, song selection, and so on. Everything else we'll decide together. How's that?"

No way. Tim wanted to be *the leader.* Across the board. "And another thing," he said. "I want to do all the talking on stage."

"You're kidding," I said. "We've always split that up—you talk sometimes, I talk sometimes. We both enjoy it, so—"

"Yeah," Tim said. "We both enjoy it, but you're no good at it. You stink, in fact. I'm better at it, so I'll do the talking."

What?

How do you respond to something like that? Let me admit, first of all, that I didn't respond very well. I went home not just discouraged but humiliated. After all, it must be true—I must be a lousy speaker. Why else would my friend Tim say so? It was, for some reason, very easy under those circumstances to forget several things—such as the awards I'd received for speeches I'd given, or the fact that I was a disc jockey, sending out my voice to millions of people every day, in Orange County, California, one of the most competitive and toughest radio markets in the country.

Over the next few weeks, I didn't say much to Tim about it. I became moody and withdrawn. I'd had a goal for that group: I wanted us to be the best Christian music group we were capable of being, and I wanted to use the talents God had given me to help make that happen. But I allowed myself to be deflected from that goal, because of an insensitive and untrue remark made by someone who wanted to impose his own goal. Tim got his way, for the most part. He got to do the talking, or at least most of it, but he didn't have much of a partner. By imposing his goal on me, Tim had damaged the relationship upon which his goal would depend.

No, that wasn't the end of Tim and Dave; we went into other partnerships later, and we're friends to this day. But it was a bad scene nevertheless, for two reasons. For one, Tim shouldn't have tried to achieve *his* goal—being the "leader" and the main onstage personality—by making me feel bad about myself, in order to control my behavior. And for another, I should have stood up for myself.

It was one of those "I should have said . . ." situations. So what *should* I have said? Something like this:

"Hey, Tim. Look, we've been friends for a long time. But I can't accept this kind of thing from you. How do I know whether this is really what you think or whether you're just saying this so you can accomplish your goal to do all the talking?

"And besides—friends just don't do this kind of thing to each other, Tim. You're trying to manipulate me to get your own way—but that's hurting *me,* Tim. Think about it. You'd hurt me to get your own way? And you call yourself my friend? Come on.

"Look, I want to keep singing with you. And I want our group to get even better than it is now. But we're not going to do that by discouraging and criticizing each other. We'll do it by encouraging each other, by building each other up. That way, we'll both become the *best* we can be, and we'll both have a lot more to offer this singing group and the people we minister to. So let's make that the model for our relationship, all right?"

By the time I'd figured all of this out, of course, it was far too late to say it. But I've definitely been more aware since then of people trying to manipulate me to accomplish their own goals, without regard for my goals or my well-being. If I haven't always been able to eloquently respond, at least I've known enough to resist.

Verse of the Day:

But make up your mind not to worry beforehand how you will defend yourselves. For I will give you words and wisdom that none of your adversaries will be able to resist or contradict.

LUKE 21:14–15

Want to know More?

Here's a great passage, in Jesus' own words, explaining why we should speak up when people treat us this way: Matthew 18:15–17.

Just Do It:

For the past few days, we've been talking about manipulation through guilt. Today's example is a little different; it's really more like manipulation through intimidation. But the two are pretty closely related; they're both ways in which people manipulate us by making us feel bad about ourselves.

This is a good time to simply spend several minutes in prayer. Ask God to give you the wisdom and mental quickness to recognize manipulation through guilt or intimidation when it's happening to you, and the strength and boldness to resist it verbally. Ask him to give you the right words—not a year later but right then, when the person is still standing before you. Because if you speak those words boldly and plainly, you might find that you've not only saved yourself from manipulation but also saved a friend or family member from making a serious mistake and enabled them to recognize a bad habit while there's still time to change it. Pray right now that God will prepare the hearts of those people who'll someday try to manipulate you, so that they'll recognize the truth when you speak it, and respond positively.

What! Turn Off My Walkman?

That's a pretty radical thought. Most of us like to have sound and music wherever we are, whatever we're doing. Maybe you're one of those people who always have the television turned on when they're home, even if they're not watching it. You just like the sound. It makes you feel less lonely.

When you're in the car, you like to have the radio turned on or a tape in the tape player.

And maybe in your devotional time with God (on the days you get around to having one), you like to have some Christian music playing. Then as soon as you're done reading or praying, you jump up and run off to do something else.

Christian music, reading, and praying are all good things. But they leave out one important part of relating to God. Sometimes he just wants us to sit. And be still. And do nothing—except wait and be still.

A woman went to a Christian retreat center to pray and draw closer to God, but she felt as if her prayers meant nothing and were going no higher than the ceiling. When she complained to a counselor there, he said, "Go back to your room and knit."

"Knit?" she asked, puzzled.

"Yes, knit," he said. "Knit unto the Lord. Don't pray. Don't read your Bible. Just quietly knit."

And so she did. After a few days of setting aside time to quietly knit, she realized that the silence that surrounded her during that time was not, as she had thought at first, an absence—the absence of sound. Instead, it was a presence.

The presence of God.

Sometimes we have to keep quiet so that God can speak to us. Not all of prayer is talking to God. Sometimes it's quietly listening.

Verse of the Day:

"Be still, and know that I am God."

PSALM 46:10

Want to know More?

Sometimes God has to go to some pretty radical lengths to get us to listen to him! Read what God had to do when Elijah wouldn't listen, in 1 Kings 19:1–18.

Just Do It:

We wouldn't expect you to suddenly start sitting completely still and listening for God for a half hour. You have to work up to it. But start small. Today, maybe right now when you finish reading this, turn off the music if you have some on, make sure you can be undisturbed for a while, close your eyes—and just listen to God for one minute. Sixty seconds. It may feel really weird, you may think it's a waste of time, but just try it.

Tomorrow do it for two minutes.

Add a minute a day up to ten minutes and then keep doing it for a while at ten minutes a day.

Don't try to pray during that time, don't talk to God, don't think about your girlfriend or the test tomorrow or the argument you just had with your dad—just be still.

We're not saying that God will speak to you, not in words and maybe not even in thoughts. The idea is just to start to tune in to the presence of God.

To be still and to know that he is God.

If you can do just that much, you'll have done a great deal.

Arnold

Dave

Arnold was the kind of kid nobody would want to be like. Except maybe in height. By the time we were sophomores, Arnold was already about six two. But that just made him feel more awkward and self-conscious, and he walked with his back a little hunched over so he wouldn't be noticed as much.

Arnold, you see, was painfully shy. He hated any kind of attention; he got this startled, rabbit-in-the-headlights look in his eyes anytime anyone spoke to him. He was smart—very smart— but horrible at sports, because he didn't have strength or coordination to go with his height. He was skinny too. And his complexion was pretty bad.

It wasn't that anyone actually disliked Arnold. Instead, we either didn't notice him at all or, if we did, we felt sorry for him.

Arnold was discovering firsthand what anyone who pays any attention knows very well about our society, and it's as true in high school as anywhere else. People are valued in society according to whether they were born with certain characteristics. Athletes have great value in our society. Beautiful people have great value in our society. Rich people have great value in our society. Really smart people have great value in our society (although smart people often have to wait longer, like till they're adults, to reap the benefits of that value).

Then something weird happened with Arnold. About halfway through our sophomore year, we had a talent assembly. You know, the kind in which the kids who can sing or dance or play an instrument or do magic tricks get up and show their stuff. Since I didn't do any of the above (I was just learning to play guitar), I was a benchwarmer in this particular assembly. And at first none of the people who got up there surprised me; I'd known for years that Doug could sing and that Sandy played clarinet and that Donna took dance lessons.

Then the announcer said, "Next is Arnold Wilson."

Arnold? We all looked at each other. *Arnold?* What could he do? He had a talent?

Arnold walked self-consciously onto the stage, with his usual hunched-over walk, looking like he'd rather be anywhere else and being careful not to look at anyone. He sat down at the piano. He gently touched the keys, took a deep breath . . . and holy cow! Could Arnold play!

Our mouths hanging open, we all sat there spellbound, not believing what we were hearing. I don't know what he played, some classical piece. But it was very fast and obviously very difficult.

Arnold—tentative, timid, quiet Arnold—played that piano like he was in charge, folks. And he definitely had our attention. When he finished and stood shyly to walk off the stage, we beat our hands together and whistled and yelled, and he blushed and hurried off behind the curtain.

Nobody looked at Arnold quite the same after that. After the assembly, people who'd never said a word to Arnold, except maybe to make fun of him, stopped him in the hall to say, "Hey, Arnold. Good job, man. Didn't know you could do that." People caught his eye across the lunchroom—not an easy task with Arnold—to give him a thumbs-up.

Did Arnold suddenly make lots of new friends overnight? I doubt it. But he found an *acceptance* and *respect* that he hadn't enjoyed before. And I'm sure that despite his painful shyness, the attention he received made a world of difference in his *self*-respect.

The word is *compensation*. What it means is that even those of us who aren't great athletes or rich or beautiful can find ways to give ourselves value in our own eyes and in the eyes of those around us, usually by developing skills or talents or personality characteristics that others value—in other words, by *compensating* for our lack in one area by making up for it in another.

But wait—don't we have value anyway, even if we can't do anything at all? I mean, doesn't God love us as we are? Didn't Jesus die on the cross for us? Doesn't our parents' love mean anything?

Yes, yes, yes, and yes. But don't we all, even if we know that, still base part of our self-opinion on how we're accepted and valued by the people around us, by our little chunk of society? Yes, we do. And therefore it's important to us to be considered valuable by our peers.

Arnold did it through music. Others do it through some other kind of art, like painting or acting or cartooning. (That's exactly why Johnny Hart, who draws the comic strip *B.C.,* started cartooning.) Some people do it through humor. Some through writing.

"But I don't have *any* talents!" you may be saying. "I can't play any instruments, I'm not funny, I'm not beautiful—why would anyone want *me* around?"

You *do* have talents. God promised that he would give each of us talents to use. But maybe yours are of a little different type, like Liz's were. We'll talk about her tomorrow.

Verse of the Day:

Each man has his own gift from God; one has this gift, another has that.

1 CORINTHIANS 7:7

Want to know More?

1 Corinthians 12:4–11 helps us to understand that just because one person has one gift and another person has another, that doesn't mean that one of them is better than the other. All are important!

Just Do It:

I want you to do the following exercise, even if you're beautiful and rich and a great athlete and the most popular person in your high school. Because life can change quickly in unexpected ways, and sometimes we need to know what resources we have available to us.

Take stock of your inner resources. What do you have that could be developed in a way that might be valued by society? Ignore looks and athletic skill for a moment. See if anything on this list is a strength of yours or maybe reminds you of something else that is:

musical ability

verbal skills, either in writing or in speaking

skill in debating—or even in arguing

artistic ability of any kind—painting, sculpting, cartooning, filmmaking, acting

cooking, sewing, designing clothes, fixing hair, or other domestic skills

mechanical ability—fixing cars or repairing things around the house

gardening or making things grow; taking care of animals

leadership skills

perseverance or stubbornness—the ability to stick to a task till it's finished or to a course of action even when you're getting lots of resistance

the ability to keep cool when everything's going crazy

the ability to resist temptation; self-control

a desire to get closer and closer to God

friendship skills; getting along with others

the ability to make people laugh

All of those things—and the list could be much, much longer—provide ways for you to carve a place for yourself, even if you don't possess the physical or intellectual attributes our society values most. And most of these abilities last far longer than physical beauty.

Identify your own compensating skills and begin now to build them for the future.

Liz

Dave

She'd never have won a beauty contest, although she wasn't ugly or anything. Just plain. Not glamorous.

She'd have loved to lose twenty pounds but never did. She was self-conscious about how she looked in a bathing suit (and, living in southern California, people spent a lot of time in bathing suits). She might have been described as "chunky."

She wasn't athletic, she wasn't musical or artistic, and her grades were average. She wasn't a leader. If she had any special abilities at all—sewing or decorating or languages or something like that—I never heard about it.

But the funny thing was, when you were with Liz, you were never aware of that long list of things she wasn't or of all the things she couldn't do. You were too busy feeling good and enjoying being around her.

She was three years older than I was, and if any of the girls my age had asked me, "What should I try to be like in three years?" I'd have said, "You should be like Liz."

Not somebody glamorous and beautiful? Not some movie star? Not a famous athlete? Nope. Liz.

What was it about her that people liked so much? For one thing, she always put the focus on others, never herself. Liz always wanted to know what you'd been doing, how you were feeling, what your plans were. In conversation, she never tried to hog the spotlight by going on and on about herself. She willingly yielded the floor to you and then tried to keep you there by being a good listener and asking lots of questions.

When you ran into Liz, her smile and her tone of voice said, "I'm so glad to see you!" And you felt that she really meant it.

She was a giver, not a taker. Her interest was in *giving* help, not in demanding it. Being around her was never tiring or draining.

Does all of this mean that she was phony, that she pretended everything was hunky-dory when inside she was in misery? Just the opposite. She was very honest about how she felt. But she always made light of her own problems and deflected her own discouragement by doing something for someone else.

Liz's personality was a beautiful form of compensation. If what Liz had to offer the world, instead of physical beauty or athletic skill or brains, was a sweet spirit and a pleasing personality, then that is what she would offer, every day, with all of her might. And people loved her for it. She was a welcome member of any group.

She could, of course, have taken another path—complaining and moaning that she wasn't more beautiful or richer or more talented. Who'd have wanted to be around her then?

Remember: God won't necessarily give you more athletic skill or make you better looking just because you pray about it. But a personality like Liz's is a personality that pleases God, and he will, through his Holy Spirit, enable you to act that way toward others, even if it isn't easy for you.

Liz's path is open to anybody. It's not likely to get you elected president of the student body or head cheerleader, but it will make you a good friend. And people flock to good friends.

Verse of the Day:

But the fruit of the Spirit is love, joy, peace, patience, kindness, goodness, faithfulness, gentleness and self-control. Against such things there is no law.

GALATIANS 5:22–23

Want to know More?

It's useful to read the whole passage of Scripture today's verses come from, because not only does God tell us how he wants us to act, he also tells us how he doesn't. Read Galatians 5:13–26.

Just Do It:

After you've read those verses in Galatians 5, do two things:

First, pray that God will empower you to live according to the fruit of the Spirit, acting in love, patience, kindness, self-control, and so on.

Next, monitor your attitudes and actions all day long today. (Or tomorrow, if you're reading this at night.) You'll find yourself, again and again, wanting to act in some other way—impatiently rather than patiently, harshly rather than gently, aggressively rather than peacefully, and so forth. Stop right there, send up a quick prayer, and make the conscious effort to act as those verses tell us God wants us to. You may not succeed every time, but your batting average will definitely increase.

And you'll find that people begin to look at you differently—as someone who really acts like a good friend, someone who treats them with kindness.

Someone who acts as Liz would.

Or as Jesus would.

Fighting Swordfish

Dave

No, this isn't a fishing story. It's a fighting story.

Among the group of guys I grew up with in my neighborhood in southern California, as among most groups of boys, fights weren't uncommon. And the fight I remember best was the one between me and Anthony Giuliani, who was nicknamed Swordfish.

Swordfish lived four or five houses down from me, and although all the kids on my block agreed that his older brother—who was a few years older than those of us in my gang and had a car as well as a pretty good record collection—was the coolest guy around, we also agreed that Swordfish was a poor imitation. He got on my nerves a lot.

So it seemed inevitable that one day it would come to fists, and when that day came, I was pretty confident. Sure, he was as big as I was, but I was a year older, presumably smarter and more streetwise, and I expected to cream him.

"Watch out," my friend Doug cautioned quietly as I set my books and lunch pail down and took off my jacket. We were still standing at the bus stop after getting off the bus, but we'd been standing and arguing so long, Swordfish and I, that all the rest of the kids had wandered on home, and just the three of us were left. "He's got quick hands."

I smirked. "What are you talking about? He's a third-grader. I'll murder him." I turned to face Swordfish. Hmmm. He did seem a lot bigger than most third-graders.

"Last chance," I said, bringing my arms up and going into my "boxing bounce." "Apologize and run home to Mama, and I won't break any bones. This time."

Uncharacteristically quiet—usually he wouldn't shut up, which was one of the things that bugged me about him—he just shook his head and moved a little closer. I decided I liked him better when he was talking.

"You'll be sorry," I said, and then this fist came from somewhere and smashed me in the eye.

I'm not sure to this day that the fist belonged to Swordfish. I don't see how it could have come from him all the way to my eye that fast. Maybe he had an accomplice in a low-flying airplane who reached out and smashed me one at just the right moment, I don't know. But it hit me hard and it hurt.

Swordfish turned out to be one of those fighters who attack fast and furiously, trying to win the fight in thirty seconds. I managed to block at least a few of his blows during that thirty seconds, and even land a few of my own, and then he backed off a bit when he saw he hadn't won yet, and we settled into the general pattern for most of the fights in my neighborhood—circling each other endlessly, trading insults, every once in a great while exchanging a few blows.

"Thought you were going to break my bones," Swordfish muttered. "Haven't even hit me yet."

"Baloney," I panted. "I've hit you plenty. You've got bruises all over your face." He didn't, actually, but unless he carried a mirror in his pocket, there was no way for him to know that, so it was a safe boast.

He seemed a little uncertain, even reached one hand up tentatively to touch his cheek, which gave me an opening and I swung for his stomach—and hit his arm instead. "No I don't," he said. "You haven't even *hit* my face yet."

"Have too."

"Have not."

"Have too. Plenty of times."

"Boys!" It was Mrs. Winters, who lived in the house right next to the bus stop. "You stop that right now and go on home. Right now! Scoot!"

Carefully, keeping a close eye on each other, we drew a little farther apart and began gathering up our stuff, both secretly relieved to have this fight over with.

"I won," he said.

"Did not. *I* won. I hit you more times."

"Did not. And anyway, I hit you in the *face* more times. That counts double."

"Only if you draw blood. You see any blood on my face?"

And so we argued all down the street, till we got to my house and Swordfish, shouting another insult or two over his shoulder, walked on.

"He got you pretty good a couple of times," Doug said. "Hurt? You look like you're gonna have a black eye. I *told* you he was fast for a third-grader."

"See you tomorrow," I told him, not really wanting to talk about it, and went inside.

I dropped my books on the couch. I could hear my mother in the kitchen, washing dishes, which in those days meant standing in front of a sink of hot soapy water and washing them by hand.

I walked into the kitchen. My mom turned around to greet me, saw the look on my face, wiped her hands dry, and opened her arms. I stepped between them, put my head against her, and cried.

She waited till I was all cried out before she asked what was wrong, realizing that the exact cause of my tears wasn't as important as my need for her reassurance. That day it was the emotional stress of a fistfight—especially one I'd thought I would win but hadn't—and the pain of the blows I'd taken (although I didn't get that black eye). On another day it would be something else. Life has its rough places, especially when you're a kid, and sometimes you just need a shoulder to lean on while you cry the tears that you would never let your friends see.

A few years after the Swordfish incident, of course, the growing pains of adolescence made me draw back from my parents. Those times of crying on Mom's shoulder were over; I was trying to be independent.

I had no way of knowing at the time how many future Swordfishes I would have to face down and fight to a draw on my own or how many different kinds of fists can come from out of nowhere and knock you silly. Well into my forties now, I've faced more than my share.

But those childhood sessions with Mom and Dad, when they absorbed my tears, caressed my little face, and sent me back out refreshed and reassured, did more than set the world of a child back on its proper axis. They reminded me that no matter what size you are, no matter how grievous the hurt, there's always someone big enough to enfold you in his arms, let you cry out your pain, and say, "It's all right. Everything will turn out fine."

Verse of the Day:

Cast your cares on the LORD and he will sustain you; he will never let the righteous fall.

PSALM 55:22

Want to know More?

Read 1 Peter 5:5–10. It reminds us to turn all of our worries over to God, as today's verse does, but it also has a lot of other great advice for living like a Christian in a fallen world.

Just Do It:

"Cast your cares on the Lord," today's verse says. But you probably don't think of that in the same way you think of talking your fears or worries over with your best friend, or the way you used to think of coming to Mom or Dad when someone punched you in the eye.

Maybe making a change in the way you bring your problems to the Lord would help. Today write God a little letter. Just pretend you're writing to a good buddy and tell him about something that's really got you sweating it. (Come on, don't tell me you haven't got any problems bad enough to keep you worried. We all do! Get honest!) Describe the situation to him, then tell him where you're afraid the whole thing will lead and why that worries you. Then ask for his help, and tell him that you really trust him to help you out with this problem somehow.

Just writing the letter will help. God's answer—whatever it is, even if it isn't what you would have chosen—will help even more. Remember: he's a lot smarter than we are, so when he chooses a different option than we would have, you can bet his answer is the right one.

Freshman Year

Ross

"Let's pull all these little tables together and make one big one so we can all sit together!" Carey laughed, and she and her friends from the freshman dorm, with plenty of giggling and talking, set about rearranging the little ice-cream parlor.

My wife, Pat, and I, feeling a little out of place, tried to help without getting in the way. This was our first visit to see Carey during her freshman year in college. Luckily, this weekend wasn't a real busy time for them, and it hadn't been too hard to talk Carey and about twenty of her friends into going out for an ice cream and Coke.

We placed our orders and settled in. Getting a conversation started was easy; they were eager to talk. For all of them, as it turned out, freshman year was the first time they'd been away from home for an extended period. They raved—usually with three or four of them talking at once—about life at college.

"It's so much fun living in a dorm!" one girl giggled. "I mean, I'm surrounded by other girls all the time! It's like having a hundred sisters—or else one big, constant slumber party!"

"And there's always something going on! You can just walk across campus to go to a movie or a football game or a concert or anything!" The parent side of me wanted to ask a little more about that "anything," but I decided to let it pass.

"And best of all, we've got the freedom to make our own decisions," one girl added. "We can decide for ourselves what to watch on TV or how to spend our time or what clothes to wear, rather than having our parents decide for us." The girls all cheered.

For the first half hour, someone listening to those girls laugh and talk would have thought they didn't have a regret or care in the world.

But after that half hour, they one by one began to admit to a problem that surprised me.

"I kind of miss—well, I kind of miss my parents," a redhead to my left said timidly. "I guess I thought they'd write more. Or call. Or something."

The tall, thin girl sitting across from her nodded her head. "I've called them a lot more than I thought I would. It's not that I want them to make my decisions for me," she hurriedly added. "I don't. But I just want to talk things over with them before *I* decide."

"I wish they'd come visit me, like you are, Mr. and Mrs. Campbell," another added.

"I almost took a Greyhound home last weekend, just to see everybody and make sure my family was OK," said another.

Is that your mental image of what life will be like when you finally leave home—feeling homesick to talk with your parents more? Probably not—you're probably thinking more about the "freedom" aspects of life on your own. But almost universally, young people leaving home suddenly find themselves yearning for a little guidance and encouragement and advice from the people who've brought them up—and also from the close friends with whom they shared childhood and their high school years. In fact, just before she left for college, Carey and I had a long talk in which I encouraged her to take along with her the addresses and phone numbers of all those close friends and to keep in touch with them throughout college and beyond.

Life is hard. And to get through it, you need support—not only the spiritual support that God provides through the Bible and the Holy Spirit but also the close, personal, human support of family and friends. Don't cut yourself off from that support. Even though you may have differences and points of tension with your parents as the time approaches to leave home—who doesn't?—don't burn those bridges behind you; you may need to cross them again later in a time of need. And please take the advice I gave to Carey: keep in touch with those friends from your childhood and teenage years! You may never again find friends with whom you share so much or with whom closeness and intimacy will be so natural and so easy.

And don't make the mistake of saying, "I have my friends—why do I need my parents?" or vice versa. You need a *network* of support, a *group* of people praying for you, encouraging you, being there for you when you need someone. If you rely on just one or two people, what happens when they're going through tough times of their own? A net that's strong enough to catch you when you fall is woven of *many* strands of strong cord.

Even if college is great for you, times will come when you need to hear the encouraging and honest voice of someone who you know without question loves you. Value those relationships. Don't let them die.

Verse of the Day:

Wounds from a friend can be trusted, but an enemy multiplies kisses. . . . Perfume and incense bring joy to the heart, and the pleasantness of one's friend springs from his earnest counsel. Do not forsake your friend.

PROVERBS 27:6, 9–10

Want to know More?

One of the best passages in the Bible on friendship is found in Ecclesiastes 4:9–12. Read it and think about it.

Just Do It:

Start building that support network right now, today, by a simple act: gather the addresses and phone numbers of all of your friends and relatives in something that you can take with you wherever you go—an address book or diary, for instance.

You may already have many of these phone numbers and addresses memorized, and it may seem silly to you to write them down. It isn't. After you've been away at college a year or two, you might forget them. And besides, friends and relatives move, too. If you have their current address and phone number written down in a convenient list or address book, it's a simple matter to write in their new address and phone number when they move.

And you'll always know where to find it.

Give at least one friend or relative with whom you haven't spoken in a while a call today, just to say hi and to keep those lines of communication open.

Do the Good Guys Always Wear White Hats?

Ross

But you don't understand!" the woman sobbed. "She was my *best friend*! I trusted her, and she betrayed me! I'll never trust anyone again!"

Sound like a line from a soap opera? It probably is. But it's also a line from life, and every day, around the world, many people are saying it. You may have said it yourself.

Being hurt by the people you once trusted is one of the most painful things in life. And like the woman who sobbed out her pain above, when it happens to us we often say, "I'll never trust anyone again! Is there anyone out there who's worthy of my trust?"

Yes, there is—as long as we realize that no one's perfect and that we all fail sometimes. Still, with those reservations, some people are trustworthy.

And some are really nasty—not to be trusted.

How do you tell the difference?

The difference is in their *character*. Everyone has character, but it's hard to define and sometimes it's also hard to judge. It's that part of us that defines what we're really made of—whether we're selfish or selfless, giving or taking, helpful or unhelpful, trustworthy or untrustworthy. The way we will behave, the way we treat other people, how we feel about right and wrong—these things are determined by our character.

Unfortunately, character isn't always as obvious as the shape of a person's nose or the color of his skin. That's because people are so good at putting up fronts. We all do it, of course; we try to hide our faults and encourage people to think that we're better than we really are. But people of bad character *major* in putting up fronts, because it's helpful to them. It's easier to take advantage of someone if that person trusts you. So you try to make people think you're a pretty good person, even if you're really only out for yourself and don't give a hoot about anyone else.

Sounds discouraging, doesn't it? How do you tell the good guys from the bad guys who are going around *pretending* to be good guys?

Why don't the good guys all wear white hats?

Because if they did, all the bad guys would go out and buy white hats, too.

Let me offer you one of Dr. Campbell's little pearls of wisdom. (And I assure you that pearls of wisdom are rare in life.) *You can know a person's true character only after you have known them well for at least two years.* That's because a person with bad character can put up a front for only so long. In my entire life, I've known only three people who were able to put up a front for more than two years. Eventually their true character breaks through.

Do you see why long friendships are so important? The longer you know someone, the more you can trust him or her. As we spend time with our friends over a period of years, we come to trust them more and more—or in some cases, to know just how far we can trust them. And the more we know who to trust, the less pain we'll encounter in our relationships.

Do you see how this principle is important in choosing a spouse? Many people choose to get married before they've spent that two years getting to know the character of this person with whom they plan to spend the rest of their life. They'll be surprised—and not pleasantly surprised—after the wedding. This is, I believe, the number one cause of unhappy homes.

And when you're evaluating someone's character, there's no question more important than this: What is their relationship with Jesus Christ? It isn't enough to simply claim to be a Christian; there are Christians of bad character, just as there are non-Christians of bad character. What you want to know about a Christian is this: To what extent is their life influenced by Christ's presence and by the wisdom of God's Word?

And let's never forget that this question is as important in our own lives as it is in everyone else's.

Verse of the Day:

Wisdom will save you from the ways of wicked men.

PROVERBS 2:12

Want to know More?

Start with today's verse, Proverbs 2:12, and read all the way through verse 22. In fact, if you want a Bible-reading project that will last for a couple of weeks, read the entire book of Proverbs! It's full of really smart stuff.

Just Do It:

Today I've tried to handle a very tough, complex issue in just a few words, and I'm sure I've left you with as many questions as answers. So let me leave you with one word that may help: *patience.*

There are a lot of people all around you who, for selfish reasons of their own, would like to lead you in directions that aren't good for you. But they don't care what's good for you, because they don't care about you—only themselves. So be patient. Be willing to wait, to "stake out" each situation, each relationship, until you're comfortable that you can trust the people involved. And be a little stingy with that trust; make people earn it. That means you'll have to be strong with people who try to manipulate you.

Here's a little exercise that may help. Make a couple of lists of the people you know. On one, put those people you know well enough to consider to be of good character. On the other, put those people that you consider to be of bad character. (It's entirely possible, of course, that many of the people you know won't fit comfortably on either list. That's OK. If you think they lean more one way than the other, then put them on that list for now.) In a month, take those lists back out and check them again. Do you want to change anyone from one list to the other, based on how you've seen them behave in the past month? Go ahead. In another month, do the same thing again.

As time goes on, notice how the heart—the character—of the people on your list becomes clearer and clearer to you. Learning to read the character of the people you know is one of life's great lessons.

The Sweetest Pain

Dave

"Daddy! Skate with me!" Sarai chirped as I tightened the laces of her little white roller skates. The rink announcer had just called a couples skate, and on the couples skates, Sarai loved to skate with her daddy—even though she could barely stay on her feet.

She was about kindergarten age. Red-haired, hazel-green eyes, fair skin with just a smattering of freckles, she was the kind of lovely, grinning imp that people couldn't help looking at when we walked by—and grinning back at. (I know, I know. This is the kind of gushing parent slop that nearly makes you sick. But bear with me; you'll understand in a minute why this part is important.)

My son Seth, in second grade at that time, was off at the snack bar, acting hyper with some friends and trying to figure out which candy to buy, so it seemed like a good time for Sarai to have me to herself for a few minutes. "Sure, let's skate," I said. The music started—some schmaltzy golden oldie from the fifties—and we wobbled tentatively out onto the concrete floor. Junior high couples skated past, awkwardly and self-consciously holding hands; older couples who'd been doing this for years glided past as if they'd been born on skates, born with their arms around each other.

And then came Sarai and me. You've watched kindergartners skate; it's more as if they're trying to stab the floor with their skates at each step. They don't glide; they stagger. Usually I skated right beside her, holding her hand, giving her one steady point of contact and keeping her from going over onto her nose. And that's how we did it this time, too, at first. Then she wanted to get daring. She'd seen some other little girl, a few years older, skating with her dad—both of them facing forward, but dad in front, with his arms reaching back, and the little girl behind, holding on to both of his hands. Single file rather than side by side.

"Can we try it that way?" she asked.

Why not? So I pulled her around behind me and continued to skate forward, holding both of her little hands, even though I couldn't see her.

So when, inevitably, she stumbled and went down, I couldn't see her, this little girl I loved so much. I only felt the jerk on both my hands as she fell, and knew that, as always when she stumbled while we were skating, she expected my hand to stay steady, to hold her up. But not this time. This time, because of the way we were skating, I was a little off balance, leaning back just a bit, and the sudden pull on my hands sent both my skates out from under me, straight up into the air in front.

And I hung suspended. Not for long; it all happened with lightning speed. But long enough for me to envision, with crystal clarity, what was about to happen. Sarai had undoubtedly pitched forward right onto her face. And that little head was right below me on the concrete, right where I was about to crash down with all my weight, smashing that red-haired, impish, sweet, sweet head right into the unyielding cement. And there was nothing I could do about it; I was moving too fast toward the floor. I was going to crush my daughter's head.

A father's hell.

My mind flashed backward in that split second to the treasured scenes of Sarai's infancy: how she looked when she was born; the sight of her nursing at her mother's breast; standing over her while she slept; teaching her to walk; and all the other scenes parents love. And it flashed forward to what was about to come: Sarai lying bleeding and unconscious on the roller rink floor, face crushed beyond recognition, pools of her blood—

And then I hit. Hard.

Right on the concrete.

Oh, it hurt. And oh, it was the sweetest pain. Because I'd thought what I would feel was the tiny head I loved being crushed beneath me when I hit, and what I felt instead was infinitely better: hard, unyielding concrete giving a lesson in physics to my tailbone.

My forward momentum had carried me just far enough that I fell inches in front of her as she lay on the concrete floor. And two sensations reached me simultaneously: the sharp pain of my insulted bones and the sound of Sarai's laughter.

"Let's keep goin', Dad!" she yelled in my ear, pulling herself to her feet by holding onto my shoulders.

And so we would. Just as soon as the pain subsided enough that I could stand again.

Not that I was complaining.

And that's the funny thing about parents. They yell at you, they put you on restriction, they don't understand what you're feeling or how things work in the world you and your friends inhabit. It's like they're totally out of touch, and so ticked off at you half the time that you figure they'd be happier if you just took off with a backpack and a good hitchhiking thumb.

But the truth is, they'd much rather experience the pain themselves than know that you're experiencing it. It really does—as some parents say when they're about to give their kids a whippin'—hurt them worse than it hurts you.

I saw a TV show not long ago in which a woman jumped in front of her daughter as a criminal's gun went off, taking the bullet meant for her daughter. It's a scene parents understand, because we would do the same thing if the need arose.

Just a good thing to know about parents.

Verse of the Day:

"Honor your father and your mother, as the LORD your God has commanded you, so that you may live long and that it may go well with you in the land the LORD your God is giving you."

DEUTERONOMY 5:16

Want to know More?

Throughout Scripture, God is so confident of the love parents feel for their children that he uses it as an example to explain how much he loves us! Read Psalm 103:13, Proverbs 3:12, and Luke 11:11–13.

Just Do It:

There's a line in a recent popular song (actually, it's in about a million of them): "I would die for you." Would he really? I hate to be cynical, but I wonder how many of our friends—even girlfriends or boyfriends—would actually choose to die for us.

I'm not trying to be critical of your friends—just trying to point out that there aren't many people who'd do for you what Christ did on the cross: bear the pain that was meant for you. Parents, usually, are among the few who will.

Keep that in mind today as you talk with your parents—even if those conversations are unpleasant. Remember that you're talking to people who have often, in the past, put themselves between you and the bullet, so to speak. Even if it's hard to express thanks or gratitude to them right now, be aware that it would be appropriate, in light of what they've done for you, to feel it.

Please Touch Me

Ross

When my son David, who's all grown up now and out on his own, was in junior high and high school, he was very active in sports. Strained muscles, naturally, were common. Ice helped, as did Ben-Gay. But the best help of all came from Dad's hands.

I can still remember the way he would approach me, tentatively flexing a sore arm or leg, slightly wincing in pain. "Strained it in practice today, Dad," he would say. "Could you rub it down?" And I would, for as long as he wanted, not just massaging the soreness out of that overused muscle but also massaging into him my tender affection. Through touch.

We need touches. That has become almost a cliché today. The concept is cheapened a little when we see someone on a commercial or in a sitcom say, "I need a hug." But we *do* need hugs and touches. It's one of the most important ways we signal love and acceptance to each other, especially in families.

It's easy with babies and young children, of course. Parents are always touching babies—carrying them around, feeding them, changing diapers. And young children love to crawl up into a parent's lap.

But when you're a teenager, you rarely crawl onto your parent's lap. Do you, as a teenager, have any less need than younger children do for physical contact with people who love you? No, you need it as much as you ever did.

Is there a danger that if you don't get those appropriate touches from siblings and parents, you'll gravitate toward inappropriate touches from other adults or peers? Definitely. That's one of the primary reasons for inappropriate teenage sexual activity and teenage pregnancy.

So how do you get that contact, especially if your parents, like many, feel as awkward about offering those touches as you do?

David's way was a good one. The neck rub or back rub or sore-muscle rub is a nonthreatening touch, for both parties. Back scratching is another. With dad, maybe a little wrestling around will loosen things up. Eventually you'll be able to offer each other the clearly appropriate and affectionate touches—the hand on the shoulder, the hug—that we all need.

I hope you have touchable, loving parents. Some of us, unfortunately, do not, for a variety of reasons. If that's the case, then I hope you have other caring, trustworthy adults in your life—adults to whom you can go for that arm around the shoulder, for a handshake, for a pat on the back, without fearing that they'll misunderstand or respond inappropriately.

Because we all need that contact.

Have you hugged *your* parents today?

Verse of the Day:

"As a mother comforts her child, so will I comfort you."

ISAIAH 66:13

Want to know More?

The word touch is often used in the Bible to imply healing or affection or close relationship, as in Matthew 9:20–22 and 14:35–36, Luke 18:15, 1 Samuel 10:26, and Isaiah 6:7. Let touch be a healing force in your family!

Just Do It:

So how do you break the ice and get that hugging and back scratching and neck rubbing started? By taking the first step. If you're around your parents today, watch for signs that they're suffering from a headache or sore neck or back. (We all have little ways we show these things—maybe rubbing our own shoulders with our hands, maybe rubbing the bridge of our nose between our eyes. If you don't know how your parents signal discomfort, start paying attention!) If it looks to you as if your mom or dad is in need of a neck or back rub, blow their mind by volunteering!

It may take two or three times before they get the idea, but in all likelihood, within a week they'll be asking you if you need a back rub, too. And if they don't, don't be afraid to ask.

This is a great way to make sure your own needs are being met at the same time you're meeting someone else's!

PART TWO

The Future's so BRIGHT You've Got to Wear Shades!

GOD HAS GREAT THINGS IN MIND FOR YOU

The Search for Happiness

A man woke up one morning and realized that he was very unhappy and had been for a long time. "My life isn't worth living," he said. "I would give up everything just to be happy—but I don't know how. Still, there must be a way, and I won't rest till I find it."

So the man set out to search for happiness. He went to the richest man in the city where he lived, and asked, "How can I find happiness?"

"It's possessions and wealth that bring happiness," the rich man said. "Just look at me! See this smile? I'm a happy man! Follow me around for a few days, and you'll see what I mean!"

So the man followed his rich friend around, and he watched him buy boats and people and houses and clothes and all kinds of gadgets. And it's true that the rich man was happy while he was finding new things and buying them. But between times, when the rich man tired of his latest toy, which he did very quickly, he was irritable and restless, and he didn't start getting happy again until he thought of some new thing to buy.

So the man said good-bye to his rich friend. "This isn't what I'm looking for," he said. "All you're doing by buying things is distracting yourself from your unhappiness. It works for a little while, but you're still basically unhappy underneath. Good luck to you—but I'll keep looking."

The man saw, in the newspaper, a picture of a society woman at a movie premiere, laughing. "She looks very happy," the man said. "Maybe she can help me."

"Social activities and fun bring happiness," the woman told him when he found her. "Being with my friends, laughing, going out to eat, one party after another—that's happiness! Come with me and I'll show you."

So the man followed the woman around for a few days. He'd never laughed so hard or had so much fun in his life! Her friends were witty and smart, and he rubbed elbows with famous people and ate delicious food and danced and then fell into bed exhausted just before the sun came up.

But as the days went by, the man noticed that she was restless and irritable unless she had some new social engagement on her calendar for that evening. She was only happy, he saw, when she was out doing something exciting and fun.

So he said good-bye to the socialite. "This isn't what I'm looking for," he said. "All you're doing by keeping a busy social life is distracting yourself from your unhappiness. That works only while you're busy and having fun, because you're still basically unhappy underneath. Good luck to you—but I'll keep looking."

The man kept looking for happiness in many different ways. He tried sex and sensuality, but he discovered that this too was just a temporary diversion from his basic unhappiness. He tried adventures and danger, like skydiving, and even though he found that he loved the excitement, he was still unhappy when he wasn't kayaking down the rapids or hang-gliding off a cliff. He even tried serving others by volunteering at orphanages and homeless shelters, but even though that was the most successful attempt of all, because he felt very good about what he was doing, he still felt a gnawing unhappiness inside while he lay in bed, sleepless, at night.

"Is there no one happy on this earth?" he cried into the darkness. "Is there no one who can show me what true happiness is?"

And then he remembered one person he'd met in his search, only one, who seemed to be happy every day, regardless of what happened to her: a little girl at one of the orphanages he'd volunteered at, a little girl who was quietly, calmly happy, even when she was sitting and doing nothing.

The next morning, he rushed to the orphanage and asked to see her. "Little girl," he said, "you have nothing. You own only one set of clothes, and those are secondhand. You don't get enough to eat in this place. You have no family. There's little to entertain you here, only a few tattered books and a ragged doll. How can you stay so happy all the time?"

The little girl smiled shyly at him. "It won't always be like this," she answered quietly. "Someday things will be better. I don't know how. I just know that God loves me and he'll give me a better life than I have now. Maybe someday I'll have a family of my own, maybe someday . . ." Her voice trailed off and she giggled. "I don't know. But whatever it is, it'll be good, because God is love. So whenever things go wrong, I just remind myself, *It won't always be like this. Someday it will be better.*"

The man nodded his head, thanked the little girl, and walked toward home. And as he walked, he continued to nod, and he said to himself,

Happiness isn't possessions.
Happiness isn't giddiness.
Happiness is hope.

Verse of the Day:

Now faith is being sure of what we hope for and certain of what we do not see.

HEBREWS 11:1

Want to know More?

Here's a great selection of verses on hope—read them and make a list of the things they teach you: Psalm 31:24; 33:18, 22; 78:7; Romans 12:12; 15:13; 2 Corinthians 3:12; 1 Thessalonians 5:8; Titus 1:2.

Just Do It:

This section of the book is filled with thoughts about hope—hope for your future, hope that things can be better for you than they are now. That's because we, Ross and Dave, feel that hope is one of the most important things about life. And we Christians have great reason for hope: as the little girl in the story said, God *is* love, and he does indeed have great things in mind for us, far better than anything we could think up for ourselves.

The man in our story today learned about hope in a round-about way—by searching first for happiness. Ask yourself the same question: What makes *you* happy? When you want to have a good time—on a weekend night, for instance—what's the first thing you think of to do? How do you feel if your plans fall through and you end up staying home by yourself?

Isn't it true that much of our search for happiness is, just as with the people in today's story, really just an attempt to find a diversion from our own restlessness and unhappiness? In other words, instead of *getting rid* of our unhappiness, we just cover it up for a short time.

Notice throughout the next twenty-four hours: When are you really happy? What brings about that feeling? When are you really unhappy? What brings about that feeling?

Could you use a little hope that things can be better?

Lost over the Jungle

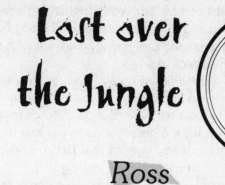

Ross

Our plane bounced along the short, primitive airstrip near the Tamarani village mission in the Amazonian jungle and lifted abruptly into the air. Dennis, my pilot, was an old hand at this, but even he looked a little uneasy—and not because of the takeoff. Instead, he looked at his watch as we quickly gained elevation. "Almost six o'clock!" he shouted above the engine noise. "We stayed too late!"

We had a two-and-a-half-hour flight back to base, and both of us were thinking right then of the main danger in jungle flying: getting lost. There are no navigational aids in jungle flying. Everything looks the same during the day: an unbroken blanket of green. The only landing strips are primitive and unmarked, visible during the day because they're the only break in the jungle other than the rivers. But because those primitive strips have no lights, pilots out at night see nothing but a sea of black.

Even leaving as late as we had, we still had some hope that we'd be able to make it back to the main missionary base, where we lived, before we lost all light. My wife, Pat, along with two of our children, Carey and David, would be waiting at the simple board home we'd lived in for the past five months as short-term medical missionaries.

But as the sun sank below the horizon and then the brilliant rose-and-tangerine streaks of sunset faded to ashes, we realized that our hopes had been foolish. With frightening speed, the remaining light faded and disappeared—helped along by a vast storm front moving in behind us—and we were left with nothing but darkness in every direction.

"This might be a good time to pray," Dennis shouted, twisting the knobs of our radio and calling into the microphone at each new setting, trying to raise our base. But only silence greeted his efforts. Finally he handed the microphone to me and turned his attention to trying to spot any signs of civilization—perhaps the lights of a settlement that might have a landing strip.

But the only sound I was able to raise on the simple radio was an annoying loud crackle. I gave up and sank back into my seat, angry and depressed. We'd been fools to take off at all; we could have stayed overnight at the village and headed home in the morning. We'd been anxious to get home because it was New Year's Eve and my wife and I were hosting a party. But our plane carried only enough fuel for the trip out and back; we weren't carrying any extra for cruising back and forth through the black night, searching for a landing strip. In other words, we either found a landing strip soon or we crashed into the rain forest.

Missing the party was the least of my worries now.

I scanned the blackness around us in the hope of spotting a light—I couldn't even see any stars now, because we'd been overtaken by the clouds moving rapidly in—but saw nothing. The fuel gauge seemed drastically lower each time I looked at it.

And finally came the sound we'd both been dreading to hear: the engine sputtering for lack of fuel.

"We're going down," I muttered in defeat. "We're going down."

Dennis's body jerked forward, his eyes glued to the horizon. "I think I see a light!" he shouted.

"Where?" I yelled.

He pointed, and I trained my eyes in that direction—but saw nothing. Was he hallucinating? And then—yes, there it was! A tiny pinprick of light, far away. We grinned at each other, but I still feared that we'd run out of fuel before we got that far.

We didn't. As we flew over it, we could see that the light was a campfire in the middle of a primitive village made up of a few thatched huts. But we saw no people, and the clearing in which the village sat was far too small to allow us to land. Many of these jungle villages, if they were permanent, had landing strips. Did this one?

"I'm not sure," Dennis yelled, "but I think this is San Jose. And if it is, my map shows a landing strip just north of here." He turned and looked at me. "We've only got enough fuel for one approach. I'm going to have to drop to treetop level and head for where I think it is. If we don't find it, we'll have to hit the trees and take our chances."

Reassuring thought.

"Let's go for it," I said.

Dennis nodded. "Here we go." He inched the controls forward and we began to drop. "Brace yourself," he said calmly, and I did. But there was no impact; instead, we saw the treetops appear just below us, as uneven and yet graceful in our lights as the waves of the sea. Dennis dropped us still lower, until it seemed to me we were about to skim the topmost branches.

Suddenly the treetops fell away beneath us, and Dennis shoved the controls forward. We plummeted toward the ground, our lights shot down into the void beneath us—and there it was! The uneven, scraggly, brushy landing strip couldn't have looked any better if it had been LaGuardia Airport in New York City.

We bounced against a number of holes and stumps, but finally he brought the plane to an abrupt stop—just ten yards away from the jungle at the end of the runway. If we had dropped toward the airstrip just a second or two later, we'd have been picking splinters out of ourselves—or worse.

"Praise God!" Dennis whooped.

"Absolutely," I sighed.

We collected our few supplies and our flashlight and headed off toward the village, about a mile away. A few minutes later we could hear, amid the sounds of jungle animals, another sound—

and we knew why we'd seen no one when we'd flown over the village. We heard hymns being sung in Spanish.

This village was in church.

And I could feel the tears starting into my eyes at this gentle reminder that despite our danger, despite my anger and impatience, despite our foolish decision to take off in the first place, God had never taken his hand off us all through this frightening and dangerous night.

Verse of the Day:

"The LORD himself goes before you and will be with you;
he will never leave you nor forsake you. Do not be afraid;
do not be discouraged."

DEUTERONOMY 31:8

Want to know More?

How should we act, then, now that we know that God will never leave us nor forsake us? Read Hebrews 13:1–8.

Just Do It:

Time for a prayer. While I was in that plane, not knowing whether we would find a place to land safely, it would have been pretty tough to pray a prayer of thanks to God for saving me from death in the jungle. But you can bet that I prayed that prayer when we landed.

I *could* have prayed it in advance, though, if you stop and think about it. Because even though I didn't know how things would turn out, I did know that I was under God's protection and care, that he had promised never to leave me nor forsake me. So my prayer could have been something like this: "God, I'm very frightened right now. But I know that you're taking care of me, so I trust you to get me out of this in the way you think best. I'm relying on you, and I thank you in advance for how you're going to resolve this."

What's bothering you the most right now? What is it that has you more discouraged or frightened than anything else? How about praying a prayer similar to the one above?

Then relax. God won't leave you. God won't forsake you. He promised.

How I Almost Started World War III

Ross

This story is going to make me sound really old, but give me a break—it's a pretty good story anyway. In fact, it's a piece of history. (Now I *really* sound old!)

I was gunnery officer on the destroyer escort *Daniel A. Joy*, stationed at Guantánamo Bay, Cuba, during the early sixties. That was a time of great friction between the Soviet Union and the United States. Several Soviet ships loaded with nuclear supplies had left Russia and were bound for Cuba, which of course was then, as it is now, a Communist nation headed by Fidel Castro. John F. Kennedy was president of the U.S., and he had demanded that those ships turn around and return to Russia. Everyone knew that war was a real possibility if those ships carrying missiles and other supplies actually reached Cuba, which is only about ninety miles off the coast of Florida.

Our assignment was to patrol the Windward Straits between Jamaica and Cuba. One blistering hot day, the entire crew was jolted by a loud voice blaring over the intercom: "All hands report to battle stations! Unidentified vessel sighted."

I scrambled to my assigned battle station on the bridge. Sure enough, I could see an unfamiliar ship off our port side.

"It's a Russian ship disguised as a freighter," the captain said. "Heavily armed, too. Wonder what he's up to." We knew that the Russian ships carrying nuclear supplies were on their way, and we suspected that this was the first of them. "Quartermaster!" called the captain. "Send a signal requesting that they identify themselves."

The quartermaster stepped up to the signal flasher and sent a message in international code. There was no reply. After a couple of minutes, he sent it again. Then we could see the Russian lamp flashing slowly. When it stopped, the quartermaster turned back toward us with a sick look on his face.

"Well?" growled the captain. "What did they say?"

His hands trembling, the quartermaster replied, "They said, 'None of your @&%$# business!'"

"They said *what!*" our captain yelled. He kicked something nearby; it went clattering across the bridge. "I'll show them whose business it is! Send them another message demanding that they reveal what they're carrying as cargo."

The quartermaster flashed out the captain's message. When the Russian reply came back, the quartermaster looked even sicker.

"Well?" the captain barked.

"They said, 'None of your @&%$# business!'"

Furious, the captain shouted, "All engines ahead, flank!" The Russian ship, you see, was newer and faster than ours, and as we'd been sending messages back and forth, it had been steadily pulling ahead. But our speed was no match for it, and we watched its stern pulling farther and farther away.

To make matters worse, Russian sailors appeared on the stern and began laughing at us as they dumped boxes of garbage directly into our path!

That was too much for the captain. "Ross!" he barked. "Load the guns! And order them trained on the Russian vessel!"

I couldn't believe what I was hearing. "Load the guns, Captain?" I stepped closer to him and talked quietly. "Captain, we don't have the authority to fire on *any* ship. And if we fire on a Russian merchant ship, we're looking at World War III here."

"Campbell," he replied through clenched teeth, still staring at the Russian ship. "I gave an order, and if you don't carry it out, you'll be facing a court-martial."

Wishing I could sink to my knees and pray, I instead reached for the ship's phone and relayed the orders: "All mounts load. All directors train on the ship off the bow." I glanced around the bridge; except for the captain, everyone there looked as terrified as I felt.

Several minutes passed without anything happening. I could just imagine the Russians watching all of our actions through binoculars, wondering whether we'd be foolish enough to actually fire. And I wondered the same thing: Would the captain, in his anger, actually give the command, "Commence firing"?

If he did, then in all likelihood, war would break out between the United States and the Soviet Union. And I would be the gunnery officer who commanded his men to fire the shots that began the war that would undoubtedly result in hundreds of thousands of deaths. I would have my place in history, but it would be a place I would regret all my life—which might not last much longer if we got into a gun battle with this better-armed, faster Russian ship. *Lord,* I prayed, *please calm our captain down—and make that Russian captain respond to our questions! We need you to intervene here, or many people will die.*

Those prayers were answered. The Russian captain decided not to gamble. He slowed his engines and sent a message via the flashers.

"They're a Soviet ship," the quartermaster reported, "carrying medical supplies, food, and hardware to Cuba."

The captain smirked. "Right," he said sarcastically. "I'm sure that's what they're carrying. Well, we have no orders to hold them, so at least we've done our job. Campbell, unload all guns."

There was an audible sigh of relief across the bridge. My knees were still shaking as I picked up the phone to issue the orders.

That was thirty-five years ago, but I can remember it as clearly as if it had happened last week. And whenever my life—or the world's situation—has seemed to be in chaos, I remember the day I personally saw God intervene, in response to my prayer, and defuse a confrontation that could have destroyed the world. And in *each* of those chaotic situations, I have seen God step in and save the day again, in many different ways—not always in the ways I'd have chosen or in the timing I'd have chosen, either. Still, I have learned to trust his power and his willingness to save us.

God is truly in control.

And he knows exactly what he's doing.

Verse of the Day:

"Call upon me in the day of trouble; I will deliver you, and you will honor me."

PSALM 50:15

Want to know More?

The book of Psalms is full of songs to God, thanking him for taking care of us, and also full of God's statements that he does indeed plan to protect us. For instance, read Psalm 3; 43:4; 72:12–14; 81:6–7; and 116:7–9.

Just Do It:

Maybe you've never been in danger of starting World War III, but we all have crises in our lives—some big, some small. Each crisis—whether it's a humongous one, like the one I told you about in this story, or something small, like locking your keys in your car—is important to God, because we are important to him. As today's verse points out, God majors in helping us out of our problems.

Today do three things that will help you prepare for the next crisis in your life. First, remember the story I told you today, about how God stepped in and averted World War III. If you're keeping a journal, write down a sentence or two that will help you remember the story. Second, remember a time in your life when some crisis that had you all upset worked out OK—in other words, when God saved the day for you, even though you might not have realized, at the time, that God had anything to do with it. Third, memorize today's verse, Psalm 50:15.

Great! Next time something goes wrong in your life, you won't be caught completely off guard. These three simple steps will help prepare you to trust that God will help you out of that mess.

And once you've begun learning to trust him, that trust will grow and grow, for the rest of your life.

Cellar Voices and Balcony People

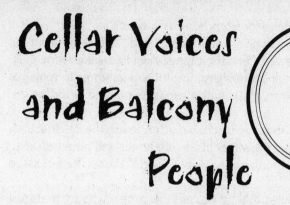

Ross

My former pastor, Moncrief Jordan, has a friend who once told him, "Sure, I often feel discouraged or full of despair. But I've found a good way to fight those feelings."

"And what way is that?" Pastor Jordan asked him, always alert to new ways of helping people.

"Why," his friend answered, "I just let my balcony people speak to my cellar voices."

Balcony people? Cellar voices? Sounds like the guy's already schizophrenic. He's hearing voices, for pete's sake.

Except that the "cellar voices" he was talking about come from two places, places that all of us share. For one, we can often provide our own cellar voices. We all have a "dark side," a basement in our lives where we keep our more negative impulses and urges: a violent temper or boiling anger or greed or lust or pride or a desire for revenge.

He did that on purpose, those internal cellar voices hiss at us. *Get him back. Don't let him get away with it.*

Or: *I don't care what's right—I'm really ticked, and I'm going to make sure everybody knows it!*

Or: *Take that away from her—it's mine!*

Cellar voices can also come from outside ourselves, from the people around us who, because of their own low self-esteem, guilt, frustration, or pent-up hostility, insult us or attempt to make us feel guilty, or try to fill us with despair about the world or our friends.

Obviously, if the only voices we listen to are the cellar voices, we're going to find ourselves filled with anger and hopelessness.

"So who are the balcony people, then?" Pastor Jordan asked his friend.

His friend smiled. "Ah, those are the people who try to do just the opposite—who try to lift us up with their love, faith, hope, and courage. They're the ones who are always telling us that we can do it, that we can rise higher than the level of life around us, that God is with us, that he loves us, that we can overcome our conflicts—inner and outer—and live victoriously.

"So when those cellar voices start to get too loud in my life, well, I just tell my balcony people about it and let them have a word or two with those cellar voices. Sometimes it takes a while, but the balcony people win every time."

Makes sense. God, after all, is a God of hope. It's not his will for us to be beaten down by temptation and despair and a depressing overawareness of our own failings. Of *course* we've failed! So what? That's why Christ died on the cross, so that we could be reconciled to God despite those failings and so that our failings could be forgiven. Balcony people remind us of that truth, just as they remind us of our value in God's eyes and of the gifts that God has given us, which we can use to give ourselves an even greater sense of value.

Balcony people, like God, want to give us hope.

Verse of the Day:

The LORD is good, a refuge in times of trouble. He cares for those who trust in him.

NAHUM 1:7

Want to know More?

Read Psalm 1. What does that psalm tell you about the "voices" we hear from the people around us?

Just Do It:

Who are your balcony people? It's important to know this, because you'll need them. Sit down and make a list right now.

Balcony people don't have to be living, by the way. People who are already dead can be balcony people if they have left behind either encouraging words or an inspiring example. Authors like C. S. Lewis or Oswald Chambers can be balcony people, or Bible characters like David or Gideon or Daniel.

Are your parents sometimes balcony people? Your friends? Relatives? Pastor or youth pastor or youth sponsor? Include those who don't live near you, too, because you can always write or talk by phone.

Keep that list. Tuck it into your Bible. Life is tough, and there are lots of cellar voices. There will be times when you'll need your balcony people to have a word or two with those in the cellar.

In fact, make it a point to talk to one of them today, just to keep those lines open.

Take Me Out of the Ball Game

Ross

"Who's the new guy?" I asked Phil, who had the locker next to mine. I was speaking loud, to be heard over the laughter and shouting of the athletes around us.

Phil grabbed his jersey out of his locker and turned to check out our new teammate. The guy was huge and built like Arnold Schwarzenegger. Phil shrugged. "Beats me. Haven't heard anything about any new tryouts. Maybe they traded for him."

We finished dressing and headed out onto the practice field. Phil and I were starters for the Albuquerque Merchants, a semi-professional baseball team in New Mexico. I played first base. I wasn't making much money on this team, but that was all right. I had a dream—my only dream, at that point in my life—and this was just one more step on the way.

I was going to be a major-league baseball player.

I had worked toward that goal for years. I'd been pretty good at baseball in high school, and I'd managed to become a starter for the Merchants. My favorite team was the Yankees; my favorite player, Lou Bodreau. Baseball was my life. I ate baseball, I drank baseball, and I breathed baseball.

Fielding practice was first that day, and I was gratified to see that the new guy, big as he was, didn't seem to be able to handle a mitt too well. But wind sprints came next, and he could run like a deer with its tail on fire. Batting practice was even worse—for me, anyway. He could hit the ball a country mile.

Relax, Ross, I told myself as I drove home from practice that day. *The guy can't field worth a darn.*

Right.

It soon became obvious that the Merchants' manager wasn't about to pass up a home run–hitting, base-stealing threat like this just because he occasionally missed a grounder. But he obviously couldn't put the new guy in the outfield. The manager started to look at me funny, and I got a strange tingling sensation down my backbone.

Sure enough. Within a few weeks, the new guy was our new starting first baseman, and I was warming the bench.

I couldn't believe it. The dreams I had cherished for so many years, that I had worked toward for so long, were being stolen from me. I worked harder on all aspects of my game; when I got the chance to play, I tried to make the big play, the one that would impress my manager. I tried to improve my speed, my quickness, my knowledge of the game, my batting . . .

And none of it mattered. As the season neared its end, I sat on the bench, watching the guy who had replaced me trot around the bases after hitting a home run. I listened to the applause he was getting, and I thought, *That's it. The guys like him will move up to the majors. The guys like me will eventually be cut. I'll never go anywhere in baseball.*

And the sad thing was, I wasn't just saying that because I was discouraged. I was saying it because in that moment of clarity, I knew that it was true.

In the weeks that followed, I struggled with two strong feelings. One was anger. I was angry at myself for not being able to play well enough to accomplish my goal. I was angry at my coach for choosing to start this gorilla who had never played first base before in his life. And I was angry at God for allowing my cherished dream to die.

The other feeling was confusion. For years, I'd had only one goal, one dream. Now it was gone. What was I going to do with my life?

When I treat patients who are discouraged and hopeless, I can sympathize with their feelings, because I certainly lacked hope during that period of my life. I was in a hole of depression and anger and hopelessness, and I couldn't see anything outside that hole.

God, of course, was not in the hole. God could see all of my life—past, present, and future—and he knew exactly what he had in store for me: an exciting and gratifying career as a psychiatrist and speaker and author, opportunities to travel the world, to serve him in exotic locations, to face danger, to raise a houseful of wonderful kids—so many things I couldn't see down in my hole of self-pity.

Do I still wish I'd been able to play major-league ball? Yes! But not at the cost of missing out on the life God has led me through in the years since then. The things I have done have been, I must admit, better than baseball.

You too have dreams for your future, just as I did all those years I dreamed of being a major-leaguer. And you may, in your attempts to accomplish those goals, find your way blocked— maybe by some gorilla who can bat and steal bases like Jose Canseco, maybe by injury, maybe just because your dreams don't match your gifts. But remember this: God too has plans for your life, and he guarantees that the gifts he has given you match those plans. And you'll never be able to find more happiness in some other life than you will in the life he has chosen for you.

Put your hand in his and let Jesus Christ guide you to the right choices for your life.

You'll never find a better guide—or a truer friend.

Verse of the Day:

And we know that in all things God works for the good of those who love him, who have been called according to his purpose.

ROMANS 8:28

Want to know More?

What can we do when life throws us a curve—when we're confused and afraid? Read Isaiah 41:10–11.

Just Do It:

I was feeling a lot of things in those weeks after I failed to accomplish my lifelong dream, but two of my strongest feelings were anxiety and worry. What's the opposite of anxiety? Peace. What's the opposite of worry? Relaxation.

If I had known how to trust God at that stage of my life, I'd have been able to relax more, even in the face of disappointment; I'd have felt more peace.

Start now learning to trust God. It's like learning a new sport—the more we practice, the better we get. We never get it perfectly, but that's OK—we can still become mature, stable, confident people.

How do you start learning to trust him? Today whenever you begin to feel some anxiety or fear or worry, read Isaiah 41:10–11, then remind yourself that God has promised to help you.

And God keeps his promises.

The Kid Can Play!

Ross

Years after my own failed attempt to make it to the major leagues, our son David started Little League. Sitting in the stands along with all of the other overinvolved parents, I watched David swat a base hit into left field and stretch it into a double because of his baserunning speed. "All right, David!" I yelled. "Way to hustle!"

I watched him steal third, evading the tag with a pretty decent hook slide. "Nice slide!" I yelled, half standing. "Great job, David!" Other parents were starting to look my way.

A half inning later, when David's team took the field, I watched him race in from left field, scoop up what should have been a base hit, and throw a slow runner out at first with a perfect strike to the first baseman. "Way to throw, David!" I screamed, jumping to my feet. "You got him!" I poked the man next to me in the shoulder. "You see that?" I asked him. "Man, what a throw! That's my kid who threw that!" The man moved away from me on the bench, as did several other parents.

But I didn't notice. I was too busy planning David's future for him.

OK, sure, I'd missed the Show—the big leagues. I'd spent my whole short baseball career in the semipros. But maybe David . . . I mean, with an arm like that, who knows . . . and that great speed . . . Let's face it: the kid can play!

I could just see him setting records all through high school, then moving on to college ball and pitching his team to a national championship. And if it takes four years to get through college, then there's bound to be an Olympic year in there somewhere! So hey, a gold medal isn't out of the question. Then a year or two in the minors, just to get experience, before . . .

In other words, I realized, as I watched David cross the plate to score another run and get a bunch of high-fives from his team-mates and coach, that I was envisioning him accomplishing all the things I had wanted to accomplish as an athlete but hadn't been able to. The things I'd failed at. Ah, but if David succeeded at them, you see, it would *sort* of be like I was succeeding at them myself. I mean, that would be my own son out there, my own flesh and blood. In some ways, I thought with pride as he grabbed his mitt and jogged out onto the field with his team, it would be even better than if I'd done it myself.

It's funny how seductive our dreams can be. I had thought that, years before, I'd got over my dreams of baseball greatness; now here I was, starting to think of reliving them through my son. But how unfair that would have been to David! How would I feel toward him if despite this strong beginning, he ultimately failed at baseball? Would my love for him be dependent on his succeeding at the sport I loved?

But it would have also been unfair to myself. How could I con-centrate on living my life, capitalizing on the gifts and opportuni-ties God had given me, if instead I was vicariously living someone else's life?

I'm not the only one who sometimes wishes he could live someone else's life, of course. Maybe that someone else is a favorite athlete. (Remember the "If I could be like Mike" commer-cials?) Maybe it's a musician whose every song we memorize or a movie star whose films we never miss. Or maybe it's just someone we know who does what we'd like to do, but so much better—like the Jose Canseco look-alike who stole my job at first base.

But it isn't God's plan, obviously, for us to trade places with the people we admire. Why? Because he has a different plan for each of us, different jobs for us to do. If I'm trying to be Ken Griffey Jr., I'm not being Ross Campbell.

And if David Campbell is being forced to be Ross Campbell, he's not doing the job God set out for him, either.

I can never be Michael Jordan; I can never be Patrick Swayze. I don't have their gifts. But neither do they have mine; they can't do what I do. Maybe you're thinking, *OK—but a lot of people want to be Michael Jordan. Who wants to be Ross Campbell?* Good point. But remember that God gives us the gifts he chooses to give us—and then he tells us that no one gift is better than another. In other words, in God's eyes, the gifts he gave Michael Jordan are no better than the gifts he gave me. Or you.

Let's learn to trust God to choose wisely for us. Figuring out what he wants us to do in life is hard enough; let's not confuse the issue by trying to live someone else's life instead.

Verse of the Day:

For it is God who works in you to will and to act according to his good purpose.

PHILIPPIANS 2:13

Want to know More?

Here's a great passage that encourages us to be satisfied with the gifts God gave us—and to be sure to use them: Romans 12:4–8.

Just Do It:

Come on, admit it. We all have people whose skill or accomplishments or fame we envy. Mentally list a couple of those people. It can be someone famous you've never met or someone you see every day.

Now envision those people. And with their pictures fresh in your mind, pray a prayer of support for them, that they will truly perceive the direction God has in mind for them and pursue it. Wish them well and ask God to guide them.

Now for yourself. Let go, in your prayer, of any of those feelings of envy and jealousy you feel toward those people and *thank* God for making you unique and different from them so that you can perform the unique job God chose for you long before you were born. Remember: your job in life is just as important, whatever it is, as the job being done by the people you envy. Then ask for God's guidance for yourself in finding the paths he wants you to follow.

Congratulations! You're one step closer to fulfilling God's will for your life!

Does God Really Lead?

Ross

You've heard people say it before, probably in church, and you might have felt confused: "Let's pray for God's leading."

Or: "I think God's leading me into the mission field."

Or: "I'm positive that God will lead you to the right person to marry."

Is all of that true, or is it just a meaningless cliché? Does God *really* lead us in this life? And if so, how? And what happens when things go wrong? I mean, if God led us here, why are things so painful and hard?

Let me assure you, from personal experience, that God does show us the way to go. Sometimes we may be very much aware that God is leading us; other times we may be convinced that life is falling apart and that we're just one step away from disaster. Sometimes the way is clear and bright and pleasant; other times it's as dark as the blackest ink. But God is there all the time, even when we can't see him.

Let me tell you a story I've seldom told anyone.

After I failed in my attempt to become a major-league baseball player, I decided I wanted to become a doctor. But I was living in New Mexico, and there was no medical school in New Mexico at that time. The University of Colorado took a few New

Mexico students into its medical school each year, but the number was small, and the competition to get in was fierce. Still, I was determined, so I entered the University of New Mexico in premed. Sure, it would be tough, but hey—I'd made good grades all through high school, so why shouldn't I succeed at this?

In my first semester I did great. But during my second semester, my grades started to slip. Then they started to *really* slip. By the end of the year, I had a D in chemistry!

I was shocked and disappointed and confused. How can you get into medical school with a D in chemistry, especially against such tough competition? I couldn't understand what was happening. I was ready to give up.

In fact, I *did* give up, more or less. This was back during the days of the draft, meaning that all men had a military obligation; if you didn't volunteer, you got drafted. I was already in ROTC (Reserve Officer's Training Corps) at the university, and out of desperation I took the exam to get into Annapolis Naval Academy.

I was accepted. Four years later I graduated with an engineering degree. Then I served four years at sea in the navy. When the time came to leave the navy, it had been eight years since I'd left the premed program at the University of New Mexico—and I *still* wanted to be a doctor!

So I applied at fourteen medical schools—and was rejected by thirteen of them, because I'd never completed premed. The University of Florida took me on, but only as an experiment; they knew that the technology of medicine was advancing rapidly, and they wanted to see how an engineer (even one with no premed degree) would survive in medical school!

And the answer was: Not so well at first. I nearly flunked out the first trimester, because my classmates had taken all of these classes before in premed; this was all review for them. But by the second year I caught up to them. Eventually, of course, I graduated and started my career.

Was I right in my desire to be a doctor, way back when I was in New Mexico? Yes, I believe so. Then, why did God lead me in such a discouraging, roundabout way to get me there?

I don't claim to know the complete answer to that question, but looking back and knowing what I know now, I think I see at least part of the reason. Remember when I started doing very poorly during my freshman year at the University of New Mexico, when I got the D in chemistry? Now I can see that it was because I was depressed! I've treated enough teenagers with depression to know how that depression shows up in their lives, and I had all the symptoms. Falling grades is one of them. Because of that depression, I would not have been able to handle the heavy academic load of medical school. Later when I had worked through the depression and was better able to handle that challenging load, God led me back to medical school.

There are two important points in that story. First, teenage depression can be serious; it can keep you from doing the things you most want to do. Academic failure is just one of the ways that depression can hurt you. If you think you might be depressed, please send me your address (c/o Zondervan Publishing House, 5300 Patterson Ave., Grand Rapids, MI, 49530), and I'll be glad to send you a pamphlet on teenage depression; it will answer some of your questions.

Second, just as God stayed with me during that long, complicated road to medical school, opening doors for me even when it seemed to me that I'd lost any chance of achieving my dream, so he will stay with you, leading you every step of the way *even when you're not aware of it.*

Life is hard and confusing. There will be many times when you'll be tempted to give up, to forget all about his so-called leading and just go your own way.

Don't do it. God's plan is to give you a meaningful and rich life. Sometimes it takes a while for that plan to unfold—but even that delay is part of the plan. God doesn't make mistakes! So remember: even when you're wondering where he is and what he's doing and why so many things are going wrong if God is supposedly in control, he's still out there working for you.

Verse of the Day:

I will instruct you and teach you in the way you should go;
I will counsel you and watch over you.

PSALM 32:8

Want to know More?

The Bible often talks about God leading us as a shepherd leads his sheep. Isaiah 40:11 is one such place. Another is John 10:1–5—remember that when Jesus talks about the shepherd here, he's talking about himself.

Just Do It:

Are you a journal writer? Some of us are and some of us aren't. But let me suggest that you start one, if you haven't already, and that you record in it your hopes, fears, discouragements, and dreams regarding what you really want to do, or feel that God is leading you to do, and what happens along the way. It will be a record of your adventures with God—and pretty exciting adventures they will be! Someday you'll look back at that record in amazement as you see how, even during the times you were most discouraged and felt the furthest from God, even during the times you felt that God must have lost interest in you and forgotten about you, he was there, quietly guiding you.

What Will Your Life Turn Out Like?

Ross

That's an easy question to answer, right? I mean, some of us have it and some of us don't. Some have great gobs of talent—athletic or artistic or social—and some of us have zip. Some of us have loads of brains, and others of us can't figure out how to open a bag of chips without spilling them all. Some of us are rich and some of us are on welfare. Some of us are beautiful and some of us—well, you know.

But it's no secret that if you have enough of any of those good things—talent, brains, beauty, or money—you'll be a success, and if you don't, you won't. Everybody knows that.

Except for one thing. I've known a lot of beautiful or talented or bright people who've been failures at life, not just personally but professionally as well. They never amounted to anything. And I've known a few people who were born into money but as adults had nothing but their wealth—no family, no friends, no successful career. They were rich failures.

In fact, if you take two people with the same amount of talent or beauty, their lives are likely to turn out entirely differently. One may wash out in life, and the other become successful—but not as successful, perhaps, as a third person who didn't have nearly as much talent or beauty as the other two.

So what *does* determine how our lives turn out?

Time for another of Dr. Campbell's little pearls of wisdom. Remember that I said these little pearls are rare? That's true. In fact, I bet that you'll run across more of these rare pearls in this book than you will for the rest of your life! And if I'm wrong about that, please write me and let me know—but be sure to let me know what the rest of the pearls of wisdom you found are. I don't want to miss any, and they don't come along very often.

Here's one: *The main thing that determines how our lives turn out is unconscious motivation.*

"Yeah, right," you say. "Unconscious motivation. What's that?"

I'll explain by telling you what it's not. Many people would have answered our title question by saying, "The way your life will turn out is determined by the conscious decisions you make." In other words, we make certain decisions in life, consciously, such as which college we'll go to or whether we'll go to college at all or whom we'll marry. And if you make good decisions, your life will turn out well. If not, not.

Good answer. A lot of truth in that. Only one problem: What determines which decisions you'll make? This may surprise you, but those decisions aren't usually based on sitting down and looking at all the pros and cons and then making what you think is the best decision. Instead, those decisions are usually based on your *unconscious motivations*. Unconscious means *out of your awareness*—things you're not aware of.

There are a number of those unconscious motivations, some more powerful than others. One of the most powerful is our *attitude toward authority*. And I don't mean toward brutal, hostile authority, either. I mean our attitude toward good authority—loving parents, good teachers, legitimate laws. And even toward God.

Some of us just, plain and simple, have an antiauthority attitude. We may even *like* the people in authority—but that doesn't mean we're going to obey them. And the person with an antiauthority attitude will automatically have many unnecessary problems in life, because their inclination is to do just the opposite of what anyone in authority expects of them.

Take grades. A person with an antiauthority attitude will unconsciously (outside of their awareness) tend to make worse grades than they are capable of, even if they think they're working at their level best. (Remember, they're *not aware* that they're resisting teachers' authority!) And it's even worse when they graduate and get a job; they'll do poor work, because now they're rebelling against their boss, who's the most convenient authority figure. This attitude can cause problems in marriage, too, where authority is supposed to be shared. And obviously, it can keep a person from really trusting God—the ultimate authority figure.

It's not hard to see how that unconscious attitude can totally ruin your life.

A person with a proauthority attitude, on the other hand, has a head start in life. That person wants to cooperate with and please the good, legitimate authority figures in his or her life. So they work to make good grades, to put in a good day's work on the job—to be, more or less, a good person. And most importantly, this person will want to please God and obey him.

Don't make the mistake of assuming that a proauthority person is a weak person, a bootlicker. Far from it. In fact, because these people appreciate and understand the importance of authority, they're the ones most likely to step into positions of authority themselves—to become the boss or the teacher or the sergeant.

So now you know. Here's something that does far more to affect how your life turns out than how beautiful you are or how well you can play the piano—or even what you got on your report card.

Verse of the Day:

The authorities that exist have been established by God. Consequently, he who rebels against the authority is rebelling against what God has instituted, and those who do so will bring judgment on themselves.

ROMANS 13:1–2

Want to know More?

Read the first five verses of Romans 13—they all talk about how we relate to authority figures.

Just Do It:

In your journal or notebook, if you're keeping one, draw two lines down a page, so that you have three columns. In the left column, make a list of all the legitimate authority figures in your life. Start with God and then include your parents, teachers, coaches, boss (if you have a job), and so on. Don't include people who try to boss you around but don't actually have any legitimate authority over you.

In the second column, list the things you could do that would please these people. Include both actions and attitudes. In the third column, list things that would disappoint these people.

Keep this list and review it every month or so. See if you can think of things to add—or things to change, things you might have been wrong about the first time.

Pray today—and every day—that as time goes by, you'll become more and more motivated to work with the authority figures in your life, in a spirit of cooperation and support, and that you'll learn to trust God more. Your future will be brighter if you do!

The Check's in the Mail

Ross

I started my junior year in medical school in 1966. It's hard to find a more chaotic time in America's history—more and more of our young men were heading off to Vietnam to fight in an extremely unpopular war, and protest was tearing apart the colleges and universities. To make matters more personal for me, GI benefits had been frozen just when I needed them most to pay my college expenses. Sky-high medical expenses for my oldest daughter, Cathy, were destroying what little control Pat (my wife) and I had over our finances. Pat tried working for a while, but that proved to be too hard on our second daughter, Carey, so she had to quit her job.

One day I stopped home between classes to find Pat sitting teary-eyed at her desk, over a stack of unpaid bills. "Our money is gone, Ross," she choked out as I came to sit by her. "All of it. And our electric bill—" She raised one envelope. "This notice says they're going to shut off our power if the bill isn't paid by Monday."

I threw an arm around her and pulled her close. "Don't cry, Pat. I'll think of something."

But Pat shook her head. I'd been promising to "think of something" for weeks now. She stood up. "I'm going to call my parents and ask them for enough money to pay the electric bill and Cathy's hospital bill for the month. Then I'm going to look for another job."

"You *can't* start working again," I said, flopping into a chair. "You know what that does to Carey. And don't call your parents. They've helped us more than they can afford already."

"But we *have* to pay these bills!" she argued.

"Just give me a chance to think of something," I mumbled, putting my head in my hands. She stood quietly, waiting. Finally I said, "I'll go by the Office of Student Affairs. Maybe I can get a part-time night job on campus. That would get us over the hump."

"But we need something to pay these bills *right now*," Pat insisted. "You can't get a paycheck in four days."

"I'll ask for an advance," I said.

Pat just shook her head. "I'm going to call my folks."

I sighed. "Give me until Friday, OK? I'll come up with something by then."

I headed out the door. How would I manage to pass my courses if I had to take on a part-time job? This semester was already hard enough. I was tempted to be angry at God, but instead I seemed to sense him trying to reassure me not to worry, that everything would be taken care of. I shook my head. I didn't have much of a choice, really. I could only do what I could do, and if that wasn't enough, God would have to do the rest.

After class, I had some research to do at the library, and when I suddenly remembered my promise to go by the Office of Student Affairs, it was almost five o'clock. I gathered my books and ran to the office, but it was closed when I got there. Great. Just great.

Pat looked at me sadly across the supper table that night and said, "Tomorrow's Thursday, but unless you come up with something by tomorrow I'm going to call my folks."

"But you can't just keep asking them to bail us out!" I insisted, my pride hurt. "They can't afford it!"

"Then, you'd better start praying," Pat said. With a sad grin, she added, "Pray first that the power company loses our file."

I came home between classes the next day to give Pat the bad news. I'd checked with the Office of Student Affairs, and there were no part-time jobs available. I picked up the mail on the way in. Most of the envelopes looked like bills. But I also found one with familiar handwriting on it—my grandfather's. I ripped open the envelope as I walked into the apartment, and two things fell out. A short note—and a check.

Pat was just finishing getting lunch together for the two of us. She jumped a foot when I yelled, "Look at this!"

"What!" she yelled, her eyes wide.

"It's a check!" I said. "For a *thousand dollars!*"

Pat took the check to see for herself. Tears came into her eyes when she realized that it was true—she was holding a check for a thousand dollars. But I couldn't see her very well through the tears in my own eyes. I took her into my arms, and we held each other for a long time.

"But why would he send us this money?" Pat asked. "Who told him we needed it? We haven't told anybody else yet."

I let her go and picked up the note. "'Ross and Pat,'" I read. "'I thought you all could use this. Hope things are improving for you. Good luck. Give my love to the kids. Love, Granddad.'"

Pat shook her head, smiling. "I prayed. Did you?"

I nodded.

"Then, this is an answer to prayer," she said. "A miracle."

And so it was. Miracles come in all shapes and sizes. Sometimes they save people's lives. Sometimes they just pay the bills.

Verse of the Day:

"Look at the birds of the air; they do not sow or reap or store away in barns, and yet your heavenly Father feeds them. Are you not much more valuable than they? Who of you by worrying can add a single hour to his life?"

MATTHEW 6:26–27

Want to know More?

Jesus had a lot to say about our bad habit of worrying about things. Read the rest of the passage, in Matthew 6:25–34.

Just Do It:

Even though I have stories like this to tell about my own life, I also know that sometimes when I've heard other people tell stories of God's miraculous actions to save them, I've thought, *Right. That doesn't mean it'll happen to me that way.*

And the truth is, maybe it won't. We can't force God to react in certain ways; he's not some cosmic troubleshooter or genie (like the one in *Aladdin*) who automatically bails us out when we get into trouble. Sometimes he wants us to struggle through certain problems on our own, because there's something he wants to teach us.

Still, in that passage in Matthew 6, Jesus clearly tells us that there's no need for us to worry. And if you're like most people, there are things you're worrying about right now. Take out a piece of paper and make a list. What are the things that are making you anxious? Money problems? Relationship problems? Worries about your future? Write them all down.

Now, if there's anything that you can do to help resolve any of those problems, write that down, too, and decide when you're going to do it. Sometimes our problems get worse just because we put off doing the unpleasant things we know we need to do to resolve them.

But there are probably some worries left on your list that you can't do much about. Pray about them. It's in our areas of greatest weakness that God can really work in our lives, so don't be afraid to simply say, "Lord, I don't have the slightest idea what to do about this problem. Can you show me what I can do? Or if you want me to just stay out of the way and let you take care of it, let me know that too. I want to believe that you can take care of my worries and needs, as Jesus said in Matthew 6. Help me to learn that from this experience."

Will the Real Hero Please Stand Up?

Dave

Who's your hero?

Ask a bunch of your friends that question, and you'll get a variety of answers. Many teens, of course, have no heroes at all. But *Seventeen* magazine, among others, asks that question every year, and the results that come in from thousands of teenagers, male and female, are pretty interesting.

For one thing, it's interesting how quickly names appear on the list and then disappear from it; the names that dominated the *Seventeen* list just a few years ago—Clint Eastwood, Eddie Murphy, Ronald and Nancy Reagan, Madonna, Bill Cosby, and Joe Montana—don't appear on it now. Yesterday's heroes are today's forgotten has-beens.

It's interesting, too, to speculate about why teenagers picked the particular people they did. Looking at the list, I'd say most names were there because of:

- fame—which also implies wealth and success
- ability—many of them do something, like playing basketball or guitar, really well

- stubborn competitiveness—which enabled them to rise to the top of their field

When Scott O'Grady was shot down over Bosnia several months ago and then was rescued after surviving alone in the forest in hostile territory for several days, he was described by many news commentators as a "true American hero." Why does Scott O'Grady qualify as a hero?

What *is* a hero, anyway?

Not long ago, I had to struggle with that question, for a practical reason. I was working on a new book series for young readers. It would contain biographies of Christians who might be considered role models—the kind of people parents would want their children to try to be like. Heroes. But *real* heroes.

Fine. Except—what *is* a real hero?

I mulled that question over for days, talked to a few friends, and came up with an answer—not the only answer, I'm sure, but one that I think works. I have begun to define heroes not on the basis of fame or wealth, not on the basis of ability, and not on the basis of success or accomplishment. I have begun to define heroes on the basis of character traits such as bravery, perseverance, nobility, willingness to sacrifice for others, leadership, integrity, and honesty.

OK, I'll admit it. That sounds a little fuzzy compared with something easy, like, "If you're the leading scorer in the NBA, you're a hero." But a lot of NBA scoring leaders have been jerks, even if they *are* rich and famous. The truth—and I think we all know it—is that a lot of the people on those lists of heroes live horribly selfish lives and treat the people around them like dirt.

I don't have the kind of athletic or musical or acting ability that's going to land me on *Seventeen*'s list of heroes. But my life, like almost everyone's, includes plenty of so-called character-building opportunities—disappointments and hardships, in other words. I would like to think that maybe, in God's eyes and in the eyes of the people who know me, I too can be a hero—not because I can hit more home runs than anybody else or because I get $12 million for every movie I make or even because I saved someone from a fire but just because of the way I live my life, just because I face hardship with endurance and with strength of character.

I don't think God called me to be rich and famous. I don't think God calls *any* of us to be rich and famous or to be a success in the eyes of everyone around us. But I do think God calls us to be heroes, every one of us—to stand up for what's right, to act on behalf of the weak and the poor and the sick and the oppressed, to speak up for God when everyone else wants to forget him, to handle the difficulties of life with endurance and patience and strength and faith.

Those aren't the kind of people most of us identify as our "heroes," I realize. But if we're wise, those are the kind of people we choose as our role models—the people we want to pattern our lives after.

Who are your heroes?

Verse of the Day:

Therefore, as God's chosen people, holy and dearly loved, clothe yourselves with compassion, kindness, humility, gentleness and patience. Bear with each other and forgive whatever grievances you may have against one another. Forgive as the Lord forgave you. And over all these virtues put on love, which binds them all together in perfect unity.

COLOSSIANS 3:12–14

Want to know More?

Want to read a real list of heroes? Read Hebrews 11. And remember that many of those people weren't considered successful at all by their friends and family. But they were heroes in God's sight.

Just Do It:

Time to think about heroes. List first of all the people you admire for what they've accomplished or for what they can do—the athletes, the musicians, and so on. There's nothing wrong with admiring someone because he or she is, in your opinion, the best saxophone player in the world. If you happen to be a saxophone player yourself, that's only natural. You know how hard that person's had to work to become as accomplished as he or she is.

Now ask yourself: *How much do I really know about the lives of these people? Do I know whether they're kind and loving toward their spouse and children? Do I know whether they're believers? Do I know whether they're honest and considerate toward others? Do I even know whether they're the kind of people I'd like to be around—or who would want to be around me?*

Come up with another list of heroes, based not on what they've accomplished or on how rich and famous they are but just on how they live their lives. Who are the people who live unselfishly, generously, kindly, with devotion toward God, with patience and endurance when things go wrong? Who are the people, in other words, who seem to be living as you think God would want us to live?

Now you have a new list of heroes.

Which list would you really like to see your own name on one day?

Nobody's Perfect—Just Ask My Family

Ross

"Fire! Somebody help me!" Chris yelled.

I turned toward the sound of his voice and immediately dropped the glass of cold orange juice I'd been holding against my forehead to help beat the sweltering summer heat as we sailed off the coast of Florida. Black smoke was billowing from the hatch of the sailboat.

"My gosh!" my daughter Carey screamed. "There's a fire in here!"

I leaped toward the aft hatch and peered down into the cabin. Chris, Carey's fiancé, was using a rag to try to beat out the flames that spewed from behind the alcohol-fueled stove. My sons Dale and David bolted out of the cabin via the forward hatch.

We were definitely in trouble. A fire aboard a boat is always a danger, of course, because if the vessel is damaged badly enough, it could sink. In this case, an even greater danger was that we were in the narrow channel just off Fort Walton, and other boats, tugs, and barges were in the channel with us. Not only was there some danger of accidentally colliding with one of those vessels while we fought the fire but we could also have run aground.

I frantically unstrapped the fire extinguishers from the bulkhead, heaved one of them down the hatch stairs to Chris, and then went down the stairs myself, shooting blasts of foam from the extinguisher as I came. For the next few minutes, Chris and I stood shoulder to shoulder, spraying the thick, white chemical foam around the entire end of the cabin near the stove—then, unable either to see or to breathe, we lunged for the hatch at the same time and bumped our heads, just like the Three Stooges.

I was not impressed with the scene up on deck. Carey was busily trying to untie the small dinghy, shouting to my wife, Pat, "Help me, Mom! Hurry up or we'll burn up here!"

David and Dale had tossed our only bucket overboard, hoping to get some water to help fight the fire. But they'd forgotten to hold on to the rope, and now they were standing helplessly, watching the tin bucket sink into the ocean.

"Stop all of this!" I bellowed. "The fire's out!"

Startled by my anger, everyone stopped what they were doing and just watched me. I poked my head back down through the hatch as the smoke and powder began to clear—and was flabbergasted. Chris and I had managed to coat everything in the cabin—the walls, the bunks, the table, the deck, the ceiling, and even the stove—with at least two inches of white foam. It looked like an explosion in a flour factory.

Outraged, I threw the empty fire extinguisher against the nearby cabinets. Then I leaped to the helm—furious that I had to do everything while everyone else just stood around like dummies—and pulled our ship out of its dangerous spin in the narrow channel.

When I had us back on a safe course, I whirled on my still-dumbstruck family. "I can't believe this!" I yelled. "Does everyone realize that we're going to have to pay for all this damage? Chris, what did you do down there? How could you be so careless?"

What was bothering me the most, I'm afraid, was that I realized that I had overreacted myself. Alcohol burns at a very low temperature, and it's easy to put out. The fire extinguishers I had grabbed had been unnecessary. Besides, I hadn't bothered to show

Chris how to use the stove correctly in the first place. That had been my omission, not his.

Nor did things get any better. In fact, they got worse. The temperatures stayed over a hundred degrees all week, and there was no air conditioning. We all got sunburned, which made tempers flare even more—and made me even more angry at myself for choosing July to go sailing in Florida.

I yelled at my inexperienced, resentful crew when they didn't tie us up to the dock correctly. I yelled at them for the way they handled the sails and lines onboard as we sailed. I yelled at everybody for everything, until finally my crew was ready to mutiny.

What's wrong with me? I wondered. *Sure, things aren't going very well, but why am I acting like this? Why am I making things worse rather than better?*

It took me a couple more days to figure out the reason. The truth is, things were going very poorly with my clinic back home. I wasn't sure how to solve those problems, and I'd spent plenty of time worrying about them. I had hoped that this family vacation would take my mind completely off my problems—but instead, those problems were making it impossible for me to relax and enjoy my family. Or to allow them to enjoy their vacation.

When I realized what I was doing, I took the only option open to me, however humbling it might be—I apologized to each one of my crew and promised to do better.

We managed to finish the trip in reasonably good spirits. But when I suggested that next time we ought to try sailing off the Virgin Islands, I'm afraid I didn't get any takers.

And they still refer to that trip as "The Great Family Sailing Disaster."

Verse of the Day:

Submit to one another out of reverence for Christ.

EPHESIANS 5:21

Want to know More?

It takes humility to admit that you're wrong and ask for forgiveness. Here are a few verses that might help: Proverbs 3:34; 11:2; 27:2; Luke 22:24–27; Romans 12:3, 10, 16; Philippians 2:3–5.

Just Do It:

The title of this piece is true: nobody's perfect. We make mistakes, all of us, and our mistakes hurt others as well as ourselves.

Think of a time when you dumped your anger on someone else. Now think of a time when someone else dumped their anger on you. Why did their temper boil over? The odds are, you don't really know the answer to that question. It probably didn't have anything to do either with you or with the situation at hand.

Here's a tough assignment: Write down, in your journal or on a piece of paper, a plan for handling it—with patience and understanding—the next time someone expresses great anger toward you. Then remember to try it the next time that happens. It'll be worth it!

And here's why. It's another one of Dr. Campbell's rare and wonderful pearls of wisdom: *True intimacy comes from resolved conflict.* The best, most meaningful relationships we'll have in life will come about because we've been able to settle misunderstandings and disagreements. Most people believe that good relationships don't have conflicts. Not true! The more we're able to resolve the conflicts we have with friends and family members, the better and stronger those relationships become!

Chuck

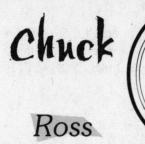

Ross

I knew—from the information Chuck's parents had given when they'd set up the first counseling appointment—that Chuck had been ditching school, that he'd been repeatedly caught shoplifting, and that his parents considered him wildly disobedient. If, based on that description, I'd been expecting a cross between Billy the Kid and Hannibal the Cannibal, I'd have been surprised. Chuck came to that first session and sat quietly, looking at the floor.

"Living with this kid is like living with a time bomb! We never know when he's going to go off next!" his mother said angrily.

"Like this last shoplifting thing," his father growled. "He'd just received his allowance—he had more than enough money to buy the stupid CD! So why did he try to steal it? It doesn't make any sense!"

As his parents angrily accused him of one irresponsible or disobedient or illegal act after another, Chuck answered quietly, meekly, with as few words as possible.

I glanced at Chuck's school records as his parents talked on. His grades had, until the past few months, been excellent; he was considered very bright by his teachers, who'd never had any problems with him before this; according to his school counselor, he was well liked by his peers.

I asked Chuck's parents to leave us alone so that I could try to get him to open up a little more. Although he was sitting quietly now, the behavior his parents described sounded like the behavior of an angry person, so it didn't surprise me that he eventually admitted to having strong feelings of anger.

"But why?" I asked. "What is it that makes you angry? Who are you angry at?"

He thought it over, then shrugged. "I don't know."

And he truly didn't. Chuck was one confused young man.

But as I continued to see Chuck and his parents over the weeks to come, some things became very clear.

For one, open and honest communications were not encouraged in their home. Chuck wasn't able to express his anger to his parents or even to discuss it with them.

For another, that same inability to discuss feelings was also causing problems in his parents' marriage. They too had feelings of anger toward each other, and since they couldn't talk about it, they found subtle, indirect ways to get back at each other—such as his mom's tendency to spend too much money, or his dad's tendency to spend as much time as possible away from home.

Furthermore, Chuck had little clear behavioral guidance from his parents, because they couldn't agree on what rules to set—or on how to discipline Chuck if he broke the rules.

Chuck had grown up as a "good kid"—someone who really wanted to please his parents and his teachers. But finally, in frustration and anger, he'd given up. How do you please people who won't tell you what they want but who are constantly telling you that what you're doing isn't good enough?

Chuck's problem, a fairly common one, raises an interesting question: Who is responsible for the problems in Chuck's behavior, Chuck or his parents? After all, it's clear that their own problems have had a definite influence on his attitudes and that he is basically a good kid who wants to please his parents. So isn't it fair to say that his problems are their fault and that they should be held responsible?

On the other hand, what good would that really do Chuck? If his *parents* are responsible for his problems but refuse to cooperate in resolving them, then what hope does Chuck have to make any positive changes in his own life? Is he doomed?

And besides, what does that do to our understanding of right and wrong? If we're not responsible for our own actions because we're just reacting uncontrollably to our upbringing, then what is sin?

There's an interesting story in the Bible. Jesus and his disciples were walking along and came to a blind man. The disciples asked, "Rabbi, who sinned, this man or his parents, that he was born blind?"

"Neither this man nor his parents sinned," Jesus answered, "but this happened so that the work of God might be displayed in his life."

And then Jesus healed the man so that he could see.

Admittedly, with Chuck, we're talking about behavioral problems, not physical ones. But the application is the same. The question is not, Who sinned, Chuck or his parents? The question is, How do we get Chuck well? And doing that may require both Chuck and his parents to make some changes. But even if his parents have no interest in changing, Chuck can still take charge of his own life and make the changes he needs to make and get the help he needs to get, on his own. In fact, Chuck's not likely to overcome his behavioral and attitudinal problems unless he *does* take personal responsibility for his own recovery.

Tomorrow we'll talk about a woman named Shari, who had a related problem.

Verse of the Day:

For we must all appear before the judgment seat of Christ, that each one may receive what is due him for the things done while in the body, whether good or bad.

2 CORINTHIANS 5:10

Want to know More?

Read the whole story of Jesus healing the blind man, in John 9:1–41. Notice that not only Jesus but also the man who was healed got into trouble with the authorities for the healing!

Just Do It:

There's a lot of finger-pointing going on these days. It seems as if everyone is trying to blame someone else for their problems: husbands blaming wives, children blaming parents, employees blaming their bosses, one politician blaming another, and so on.

The blame game is a dangerous one to play. Take a few minutes today to take stock of your own situation. Are you blaming anyone for your attitudes and behavior? If so, then pray for the strength to admit your own responsibility for yourself, and pray for the wisdom to think and act more appropriately in the future.

"I Made It— And They Can, Too"

Dave

Imet Shari when I was fresh out of college, working at my first "real" job. At first I was aware only that she was small, friendly, a little quiet—maybe even timid—but also well able to stand up for herself when she needed to. She had a college degree; without it, she'd never have got the job. And she was good at her job, too.

When Shari found out that I was a volunteer Young Life leader, she had some questions about it—so many questions, in fact, that we ended up sitting in my office long after quitting time one day, just talking.

She asked whether we had any hard-to-reach kids in our program, any substance abusers or kids in trouble with the police. "A few," I said. "But you wouldn't believe the backgrounds some of them come from. I've been in those homes. Their parents are worse than the kids are. It's hard to imagine how the kids could have turned out any differently, coming from—"

"Stop it!" Shari said angrily.

I blinked. "Stop what?" I asked.

"Stop making excuses for those kids! That's the last thing they need. You should hold them to the same standards you would any other kid. Just because they've got it rough at home doesn't give them any excuse to become addicted or to behave like criminals."

Wow. Harsh words from little Shari. And she looked as if she meant it, too. There was fire in those eyes.

I stepped around the corner to the pop machine and got us a couple of cans. "Now," I said, handing hers to her. "Mind telling me why this is such an emotional topic for you?"

She sipped her pop, waited for a minute or two, and then said, "Both my parents were alcoholics. My sisters and I never really knew what kind of mood they'd be in. They'd be fine one day, then beat on each other—or us—the next. We never had money for food. My mom was sound asleep most of the day or else just gone, and if she was home, she'd be too blasted to shop or cook anyway. I was the oldest, so I did the shopping for my sisters and me when I could find enough change in my parents' pockets.

"Our house—" Shari shook her head. "Thick layers of dirt and grease and dried vomit everywhere; garbage and empty bottles ankle-deep in every room. At first my sisters and I tried to keep it clean, but finally we gave up; it was hopeless. I went through school without anyone ever finding out where I lived.

"But school was horrible anyway, because our clothes were worn out and too small, of course, and everybody made fun of us. Church wasn't any better. Every now and then my parents would send us to Sunday school on the church bus. But besides our clothes, we never had money for the offering plate, and we never had those little workbooks that all the other kids in the class had. So we hated it." She looked up at me, some bitterness still showing in her eyes. "That was *my* introduction to Christianity."

"I never realized," I said, shaking my head. "I'm sorry—"

"Don't be sorry," she answered forcefully. "Just listen. I could have used all of that as an excuse to become someone just like my parents. I could have started drinking. I took the opposite approach. Because I didn't want to repeat their mistakes, I never took a drink at all. Instead of wasting my life, I was determined to make something of myself. So I worked my way through college, since I couldn't count on any financial help from my parents. And rather than allowing myself to become a moral failure, I've maintained even higher moral standards for myself than most people. And my sisters have done the same."

She set her empty pop can on the table. "So you want to know what to do for the kids in your group who come from backgrounds like mine?" she asked. I nodded. "Then, treat them like you would any other kid, except with maybe an extra measure of encouragement and love and support. But don't—*don't*—give them any excuses. Don't feel sorry for them. Hold them accountable. Hold them personally responsible for their own behavior. Help them see that the parent is responsible for the parent's behavior, and the kid is responsible for the kid's behavior.

"Don't coddle them. Life is tough, and their life will be tougher than most. They'll need to be strong to get through. Don't fool them into thinking you're some kind of crutch for them, because you won't always be there."

Then she smiled. "But look at me. I made it. And they can, too."

Verse of the Day:

There is surely a future hope for you, and your hope will not be cut off.

PROVERBS 23:18

Want to know More?

Just because you find yourself in a bad situation doesn't mean things can't get better. Think about Joseph—sold into slavery by his brothers after they decided not to kill him (talk about a dysfunctional family!), he was then falsely accused by his owner and thrown into prison! But read what happened next, in Genesis 41:1–43.

Just Do It:

I include Shari's story here because I'm aware that not everyone grows up in the "typical American family"—two parents, two cars, a house in the suburbs, and so on. In fact, that kind of family is rapidly becoming a minority. I grew up in one, but my own kids have lived in a bewildering variety of situations, from single-parent homes to stepfamilies.

Maybe your home situation is more like Shari's. Maybe your parents have some significant problems. And I'm not talking about the normal problems that crop up between parents and teens—difficulty in communication, eruptions of anger, and so on. I'm talking about addictions of one kind or another, or a criminal lifestyle, or serious emotional disturbance.

Or maybe you don't live with your parents at all.

It's easy, in those harsh situations, to decide that you just don't have a chance to make anything of yourself, that the cards are stacked against you from the start. It's easy to just give in to the destructive lifestyles that are all around you: gangs, substance abuse, sexual promiscuity.

Don't do it. Remember Shari. Life is tough for everybody. Your life, like Shari's, may be harder than most. Don't use that as an excuse to let your life go down the drain.

Take some practical steps right now to give yourself a better chance. For one, identify at least one caring adult who can help you when things get rough: a teacher, a youth pastor, a neighbor, a school counselor, a relative. Make a call to that person today and talk this over with them. Then spend some time talking it over with the one person who can do more to help you than anyone else: God.

Shari made it. You can, too.

Where's Dale Now?

Dave

My daughter Sarai struggled with a lot of behavioral problems in her midteens: running away, substance abuse, problems in school, and so on. We tried several residential treatment programs; she spent fourteen months in one of them, a program called Straight, before she finally overcame those problems. It was while she was in that program that we met Dale, another participant in Straight.

Like almost all the kids in that program, Dale was there against his will. "I don't belong here!" he would scream. "I'm not a drug addict!"

But aren't you using marijuana, inhalants, cocaine, LSD, and a long list of other drugs, Dale? And don't you come home drunk several nights a week?

"Who says? You can't prove it! And besides, I can handle it. Drugs don't control me; I control them."

Sure, Dale. But haven't you been arrested twice in the past month for stealing so that you'd have the money to buy these drugs you say don't control you? And aren't you failing all your classes at school, because you hardly ever show up? And didn't you pull a knife on your mother the other day? And doesn't your car have a couple of bullet holes in it from some outraged "friend" who tried to kill you? It sounds to me as if your whole life is out of control, Dale.

"That's not true! And besides, it's not my fault anyway. It's my parents. They're crazy! My dad thinks he's still in the marines. He's not real; he's made out of tin or something. And my mom's a lush. You talk about *me* being an addict; ask her how many Valiums she pops in a day!"

In Straight, we were used to kids blaming all their problems on other people, especially parents. And in many cases, they had a point. Dale's parents, for instance, were pretty much as he described them.

Was Dale justified in saying that some of his problems sprang from his home life and from his parents' influence? I'd have to say, having met and talked with them, that he was. Was he justified in blaming his *behavior* on his parents? No. We're all responsible for the choices we make, and Dale had made some bad choices. He could have chosen other, better options.

But practically speaking, that isn't the real question. The question is not, Can Dale blame his parents for his problems? The question is, What's the best way for Dale to get better so that he can have a life for himself? And the answer is, Dale needs to take responsibility for his own problems and make what changes he needs to make in his attitudes and habits so that he can function in society. Because obviously, if he keeps up as he has been, he's going to end up either in prison or with a bullet through his head.

Maybe if Dale had made that wise choice, his parents would have found the strength and wisdom to help him in reclaiming his life from the mess it had become. Maybe not. After several months of loudly and bitterly blaming his parents for everything from his height (he was short) to his anger and his drug problem and his lousy record at school and his losing his girlfriend and his troubles with the law, Dale managed to run away from Straight. We never heard from him or his parents again.

The tragedy in that story is that Dale had a great opportunity to make himself healthy again, and he refused it. He was simply unable, or unwilling, to make the simple statement that would have enabled him to start regaining control over his life: "Wherever the problems in my life came from, they're *my* problems, because it's *my* life. If I don't want those problems to destroy me, then I've got to take responsibility for them and get what help I need to solve them, and I can't let anybody or anything stand in my way."

My daughter, fortunately, was able to make that statement, as were several of the other kids in the program. Those who understood that simple truth emerged from the program in control of their lives. Those who didn't, like Dale, washed out.

Who takes the responsibility for *your* problems?

Verse of the Day:

The son will not share the guilt of the father, nor will the father share the guilt of the son. The righteousness of the righteous man will be credited to him, and the wickedness of the wicked will be charged against him.

EZEKIEL 18:20

Want to know More?

Did you read part of Joseph's story in yesterday's "Want to Know More" section? Joseph could have ended up very bitter at his brothers for, first, trying to kill him, and then for selling him into slavery. But read how Joseph greeted them when they were finally reunited: Genesis 45:1–28.

Just Do It:

Keep close tabs on your thoughts today. When something goes wrong, do you find yourself mentally casting blame in all directions but accepting little or none yourself? That's not a healthy way to live. The fact is, what you accept no responsibility for, you have little control over. You begin to see yourself as a victim, someone whose whole life is controlled by the people or circumstances around them.

Wouldn't you rather be a victor than a victim? If so, then make that decision today. If you keep a journal or a diary, write it down in today's entry, something like this: "I've made a decision today. I'm going to stop blaming other people for what goes wrong in my life and simply accept the responsibility for fixing those problems myself, regardless of how they were caused. After all—it's my life! Who's going to make sure it goes well, if not me?"

Good decision! Congratulations!

"Be Strong and Courageous"

Get the picture:

Moses, the man who'd led the Israelites out of Egypt, where they'd been held captive as slaves for many, many years, and who'd led them across the desert for forty years, had died. Now they had a new leader: Joshua. His job would be to lead the Israelites into battle against the people already living in Canaan, the "Promised Land." God had given the Israelites the land, all right, but they would have to go in with drawn swords to claim it. And it would take them many years.

So the first thing we see in the book of Joshua in the Bible is God calling Joshua aside to talk to him alone. "As I was with Moses, so I will be with you," God said. "I will never leave you nor forsake you."

And then God spoke these important words: "Be strong and courageous." Just to make sure Joshua didn't miss the point, God went on to say those same words two more times in that little talk. In fact, he once said, "Be strong and *very* courageous."

Then Joshua went back to the people and told them what God had said, and they replied, "Whatever you have commanded us we will do, and wherever you send us we will go." And then they added these words: "Only be strong and courageous!"

Be strong and courageous. Interesting that what the Israelites said to Joshua was the same thing God had said to him. They knew that they would need a courageous, confident leader who could not only fight fearlessly on the battlefield but also keep the people's spirits up when they got discouraged.

God may not have called you to lead a vast army into battle. (Then again, maybe he has.) But whatever God's will for you is, you'll probably need strength and courage to obey it. Tried to tell your friends or your parents about Jesus lately? Not easy, is it? Tried to resist your friends when they want to do something that you, as a Christian, just don't think is right? *Definitely* not easy. We, like Joshua, need to be strong and courageous—*very* courageous—because God has some tough things lined up for us.

But what if you don't *feel* strong and courageous? What if you're afraid that when the time comes to make a stand, you just won't have what it takes?

Let us make a guess here: We'd guess that Joshua didn't always feel strong and courageous, either. We'd guess that sometimes when he saw the enemy army rushing across the desert toward him, waving their spears and yelling at the top of their lungs, he wanted to turn and run himself. But instead of stepping backward, he stepped forward. He *acted* as if he had the courage to move ahead, because he made a simple decision: he would trust God to enable him to complete the job at hand—even if he, Joshua, didn't feel as if he were capable of doing it.

God honored that simple faith; under Joshua, the Israelites did indeed conquer Canaan.

And so pleased was God with Joshua for his faith and willingness to obey, for his choice to be strong and courageous even when he didn't feel like it, that he gave Joshua another great honor in the name chosen for him.

Joshua is another form of the name *Jesus*.

Verse of the Day:

"Be strong and courageous. Do not be terrified; do not be discouraged, for the LORD your God will be with you wherever you go."

JOSHUA 1:9

Want to know More?

Read the whole first chapter of Joshua; it isn't long. Count the number of times the words "strong" and "courageous" occur in that chapter. Do you think God's trying to make a point?

Just Do It:

Talk today to two or three adult Christians you know—maybe your parents, maybe your youth pastor or youth group sponsors—and ask them which things in their Christian life have been the hardest, which things have required the most strength and courage. (Tell them first about what you've read in the first chapter of Joshua, so they'll know what you're getting at.) You'll probably get a wide variety of responses, but one thing should be clear: life is *full* of things that require strength and courage, and sometimes we just don't feel that we have enough of those things to meet the challenges placed before us.

Before you finish talking with those adults, ask them to pray with you that you will believe God's promise to be with you, to never forsake you, and to provide the strength and courage you need to do his will.

Be strong and courageous!

See You at the Pole— Or Maybe Not

Have you ever heard of "See You at the Pole"?

Yes? No? Well, it's a program, sponsored by several youth ministry organizations around the country, that encourages high school students to gather around their school flagpole one day in September to pray for their classmates. It's a great idea but it takes guts. If you're one of the ones who have done it, congratulations. If you haven't yet, we encourage you to do it next September.

But wouldn't it be embarrassing if the big day came, you showed up at your school flagpole that morning to meet the rest of the Christians and pray—and nobody else showed up? What would you do?

That's what happened to one high schooler in California. The activity had been announced to a couple of Christian clubs on campus, as well as to the youth groups at several local churches, so she expected that there would be a few other Christians meeting with her that morning. Can you imagine what was going through her mind when she got there and found no one who looked even remotely as if they were praying? *I'm just early,* she probably thought. *They'll be here soon.* Five minutes later when no one else had come, she probably started asking herself, *Did I get the day wrong? Is it next week?* And five minutes after that, she may have started slowly walking past the benches surrounding the flagpole, asking some of the students sitting there eating candy bars, "Are you here for the—you know?"

But nobody was. It was her. Just her.

And she could have walked away. Nobody would have blamed her. It's what most other people would have done. Not her fault nobody else came. She did her part. She showed up, at least.

But showing up wasn't what she had come to do. She had come to pray for her school. So when it became obvious that no one else was coming, she walked up to the flagpole, ignoring the curious students around her, bowed her head, closed her eyes—and prayed.

School would be starting in just a few minutes. Most of the students were on campus already, and many of them had to walk right past the flagpole on their way to class. And when they did, on that particular morning they saw one girl, alone, standing by the flagpole with her head bowed and her eyes closed.

We can just imagine the chatter among those students as they walked past.

"What's she doing?"

"Don't know. She lose a contact?"

"She's not looking for anything; her eyes are closed."

"Hmmm. You don't suppose . . ."

"She wouldn't really be . . ."

"I mean, she's got her head bowed. Could she be . . ."

"NAAAH. Not at school. That's against the law, isn't it?"

No, it's not against the law. And at that school on that day, one girl stood alone and prayed for all of those curious students walking around her.

It took guts. She knew, for instance, that all through that day and for days to come, her friends and acquaintances would be asking her, "So—the prayer thing. You do that all the time? Are you going to, like, be a missionary or something?"

And she knew, too, that there'd be no hiding from that point on. Everybody would know that she was a Christian—not just somebody who goes to church on Sunday with her parents once in a while but somebody who really *believes* all that stuff, somebody who actually reads the Bible and tries to do what it says.

Somebody whose Christianity means something to her.

We like that story. Not just because it's inspiring and true but because it points out for us one of the most important—but scary—parts of being a Christian: sometimes you have to take a stand for Christ all alone. Not in a whole gang of fellow believers but all alone. Every eye on you. Nobody backing you up. Solo.

Scary, huh?

But it happens. And that's when you start asking yourself the hard questions: *Do I really believe this? Am I really sold out for Christ, or am I just hanging around the youth group because my friends do? Do I truly believe that Christ is a living person who knows what I'm doing right now, or do I think deep down that it's all just a myth?*

It would be easy in that situation to decide that maybe being a Christian is just too hard at that moment—and slip quietly into the stream of students heading to class.

It would be easy, when you're all alone, to be ashamed to stand up for Jesus Christ.

Verse of the Day:

I am not ashamed of the gospel, because it is the power of God for the salvation of everyone who believes.

ROMANS 1:16

Want to know More?

Another good passage that talks about reasons not to be ashamed of Jesus Christ is 2 Timothy 1:8–12. And here's another good reason: Matthew 10:32–33.

Just Do It:

The last thing we would want—and we think the last thing you would want, too—is to be ashamed of Jesus Christ. But let's face it, it's often hard to identify yourself as a Christian when you're surrounded by people who think that Christianity only belongs in church or that it's all pretty stupid.

Challenge yourself. Do two things today. First, pray for the strength to be a *bold* Christian, someone who's not ashamed of the gospel.

Second—you knew this was coming—look for an opportunity today to stand up for Jesus Christ, to identify yourself as a Christian, and to do it proudly and without shame. Maybe you can witness to a friend who doesn't know Christ. Maybe when someone else is speaking against him, you can speak up *for* him. Maybe it can be something as simple as bowing your head to pray before you eat at school or in a restaurant.

The opportunity will be there.

Will you—like the girl who prayed all by herself at the flagpole—be willing to seize it?

"The Possibilities Are Infinite!"

Dave

"I've already been able to move out of my parents' house into an apartment of my own," the young man said enthusiastically—in fact, everything about this fellow seemed to be enthusiastic.

I was listening to a report, on the radio, about the auto industry in Detroit. The reporter was interviewing a number of workers in a General Motors plant, including this twenty-one-year-old.

"And I've got a car of my own now—a brand-new car! I'm making more money per hour than I ever thought I'd make; I'm saving some each month for the things I want to buy . . . I mean, think about it—the possibilities are infinite!"

I laughed out loud, thinking, *I'll bet there are hundreds of people working in that same plant, most of them probably making more money by far than he is, who look at their paycheck and say, "How am I going to make ends meet? How can I pay my bills with this? I need a raise!" But this young man looks at his paycheck and says, "The possibilities are infinite!"*

And then it occurred to me that there was one very important reason that this young man was so happy and grateful for his paycheck, that he could see unlimited potential in the life stretching before him. Guessed it yet? That's right! He's *young*! He *has* a lot of life stretching before him yet! And it can still be whatever he wants to make of it. The paycheck he sees on Friday is just the beginning; in twenty years, who knows—he could be president of the company!

But his coworkers who are already forty-five years old and are still working on an assembly line in a factory see the future a lot differently. They've already (they think) wasted their chance to make something important of themselves. But this twenty-one-year-old fireball still has that chance, and he intends to make the most of it.

Will he succeed? Who knows? All of us know, deep down, that this young man will sooner or later experience many of the same disappointments and failures that his middle-aged coworkers have already had to face. But he can still be excited about his future— and as a matter of fact, so can his coworkers, regardless of how old they are or how disappointing their lives have been—if he keeps one very important thing in mind: the most important thing about our development is not how successful we become in our professional life but how successful we are at developing our character.

Who we are is more important than how high we climb.

God has great things in mind for each of us. Some will achieve remarkable success in politics or science or the arts; others will become unsung heroes—great successes, not in their profession but as parents or pastors or Sunday school teachers or prayer warriors or encouragers. Following God's leading will put some of us at the top of our profession or right smack in the public eye; God will give others a hidden, backseat role—but it will be no less important. Each of us, in some area of life, has a very important role to play in God's grand scheme of things; each of us, in some area of life, can be a hero—whether anyone ever knows it or not.

Each of us is destined for greatness.

We can accept that destiny, even though we might not yet know what it is, by yielding ourselves to God and agreeing to walk through the doors he opens for us when he opens them.

Or we can reject it and settle for mediocrity.
But why do that . . .
. . . when the possibilities are infinite?

Verse of the Day:

I can do everything through him who gives me strength.

PHILIPPIANS 4:13

Want to know More?

Here are a couple more passages that remind us that nothing is impossible with God: Matthew 17:20–21 and Luke 18:23–27.

Just Do It:

Do something definite today to move toward the things you want to accomplish in life.

Just choose one of your dreams and decide on one step, just one, that will help bring you closer to making that dream a reality. It could be writing away for the catalog of the college you want to go to or checking a book out of the library to help you develop a skill you'll need or calling someone who is already successful in that field to see if they'll give you some help or advice. It's not important which step you take today; what *is* important is to begin the habit of working toward your goals regularly. The possibilities are infinite—and as time goes by, you'll get a clearer and clearer picture of what God has in mind for you and of what talents and abilities he has given you to exploit.

But moving toward your goals takes work and initiative. Show some today.

PART THREE

JOIN
the Revolution

**YOU REALLY CAN
CHANGE THE WORLD**

Roaring
Lambf

Dave

Do you know who the Amish people are? (You do if you've ever seen the movie *Witness,* starring Harrison Ford.) The Amish are a religious group who don't like to use anything modern. They ride around in horse-drawn buggies, farm for a living, don't use any modern tools or conveniences, and wear very plain, old-fashioned clothes that they make themselves.

Their version of religion is to keep as far away from the rest of the world as they possibly can and to make themselves completely different from it, because they believe it's evil.

My friend Bob Briner wrote a book called *Roaring Lambs,* in which he presents a completely different view of what Christians should be like in the world. Bob believes that rather than fleeing from the world and hiding in little isolated communities of people who act and look and believe the same way we do, we should make our presence felt in the world. He believes that we should take advantage of the opportunities all around us to be a force for *good*—to speak out, or act, on behalf of biblical values.

Bob's idea of a Christian, in other words, is not that we should huddle off in a corner and ignore what's going on in the world. Bob's idea of a Christian is that we should be standing right in the middle of where things are the worst, shouting, "Hey! There's a better way! Stop messing around and start following God!"

Sounds scary, but think about it. In the Sermon on the Mount (you'll read more about that tomorrow), Jesus said that we should be the salt of the earth, and the light of the world. What did he mean? One thing is obvious: if the salt tastes just like the rest of the stew, it isn't any good. To work, salt has to taste *different* from the rest of the stew.

Likewise, if the light looks just like the dark, it's useless. Light has to be *bright* when everything else is dark, to be worth anything.

In other words, what the world needs most isn't a bunch of Christians who are so much like everybody else that you can't tell them from the Buddhists or the atheists or the people who just don't believe anything. What the world needs most is Christians who taste as different from everybody else as salt does from beef, who look as different from everybody else as a lamp does from the darkness.

The world needs us, folks. And it needs us to be different. That doesn't mean that we have to wear odd clothes and live on a farm with no TV set. But it does mean that the people we know should be able to say, "They're different. They're Christians. They really live by their beliefs."

Verse of the Day:

"You are the salt of the earth. But if the salt loses its saltiness, how can it be made salty again? It is no longer good for anything, except to be thrown out and trampled by men."

MATTHEW 5:13

Want to know More?

Read the whole passage today's verse is taken from; Jesus had some important things to say about how we act in the world: Matthew 5:13–16.

Just Do It:

You've probably heard that old question, *If you were on trial for being a Christian, would there be enough evidence to convict you?*

I'm not trying to point fingers right now, so don't start getting defensive or feeling guilty. I'm just saying that each of us has opportunities to impact the world for good—are you taking advantage of the opportunities that are open to you? Are you making your Christian presence felt in the world around you?

Are there people you know who need a compassionate response? Wrongs you see around you that need to be pointed out? Friends who are doing wrong things and who need to be challenged to straighten up? People who need help in finding the way to get their needs met? Unsaved friends or family members who need to hear about Christ? Jobs at your church that are going undone because there's no one willing to do them?

If Jesus is our shepherd, then obviously we're the lambs. Don't be a timid, bleating lamb—be a *roaring* lamb! Make your presence felt today!

Would Jesus Be Ticked Off at These Guys?

Dave

Several years ago I was asked to speak to a group of Christian businessmen at a luncheon. (A "luncheon" is what adults call it when they get together to eat lunch. Don't ask me why.) I decided to talk about one of my favorite Bible passages, Matthew 5, 6, and 7: Jesus' Sermon on the Mount.

Even if you've never read those chapters, you've heard parts of them, because the Sermon on the Mount is one of the most famous parts of the Bible. Do these verses sound familiar?

"Blessed are the meek, for they will inherit the earth" (Matthew 5:5).

"Do not resist an evil person. If someone strikes you on the right cheek, turn to him the other also. And if someone wants to sue you and take your tunic, let him have your cloak as well. If someone forces you to go one mile, go with him two miles" (Matthew 5:39–41).

"Love your enemies and pray for those who persecute you" (Matthew 5:44).

And it's also from Jesus' Sermon on the Mount that we get the Lord's Prayer: *"Our Father in heaven, hallowed be your name . . ."*

So I ate my lunch and then stood up to talk to those businessmen—lawyers, government employees, men who owned their own businesses, doctors, farmers—expecting them to respond very positively to this famous section of the Bible.

"'Give to the one who asks you, and do not turn away from the one who wants to borrow from you,'" I read out loud from my Bible, and when I looked back out at the group, I noticed that Dan, a banker, smirked at me. *Guess he wants to reserve the right to turn away anyone he perceives as a bad credit risk,* I thought.

Then I read, "'Settle matters quickly with your adversary who is taking you to court. Do it while you are still with him on the way, or he may hand you over to the judge.'" Dennis, a lawyer, leaned across the table to his law partner, Greg, and loudly whispered, "We'd be out of business!" The men around him laughed uneasily.

"'Do not store up for yourselves treasures on earth,'" I read, "'where moth and rust destroy, and where thieves break in and steal. But store up for yourselves treasures in heaven, where moth and rust do not destroy, and where thieves do not break in and steal. For where your treasure is, there your heart will be also.'"

Several very wealthy men in the room glared angrily at me. I obviously wasn't making many friends here today.

But I pressed on: "'No one can serve two masters. Either he will hate the one and love the other, or he will be devoted to the one and despise the other. You cannot serve both God and Money.'" Ooops! That was even worse. I was afraid to look at the rich guys after that.

When I finished speaking, I managed to escape before they lynched me, but I was never asked to speak before *that* group again.

I drove home with two thoughts in my mind. First, the Bible is a dangerous book. God's truth challenges us right where we live, and it doesn't mince words. It's a brave man or woman who can open its covers without flinching.

And second, we clearly live in a society that operates according to principles that are just the opposite of the instructions God gives us in the Bible. The "standard operating procedure" of the businessmen at that luncheon really doesn't differ much from the principles of athletes trying to win a game, or kids out on the playground: try to outsmart your competitors, stay one step ahead of them, take advantage of their weaknesses, show them no pity, because if you lose, they'll show none to you; crush your enemies.

Christ preaches a different set of principles in the Sermon on the Mount: live by mercy and love, turn the other cheek, go the extra mile, don't waste your time accumulating wealth, because that's not what really matters; *love* your enemies.

Someone once said that we Christians live like aliens in a strange land, where the customs and values are opposite from our own. How true.

The challenge is to keep our own Christian values intact and not allow them to be polluted by the "alien" values of the world in which we live.

And don't be fooled: that's not an easy task.

Verse of the Day:

Dear friends, I urge you, as aliens and strangers in the world, to abstain from sinful desires, which war against your soul. Live such good lives among the pagans that, though they accuse you of doing wrong, they may see your good deeds and glorify God on the day he visits us.

1 PETER 2:11–12

Want to know More?

Check out Luke 6:32–36, another account of the Sermon on the Mount. Notice how he compares the way Christians are to behave with the way "sinners" behave.

Just Do It:

The Sermon on the Mount is *long*—three whole chapters. I'm not going to ask you to read the whole thing. But try to remember the parts I quoted in the story above, and also the part you read in Luke in the "Want to Know More" section. As you go through the day today, notice how many times the people around you act entirely different from the way Christ is asking us to live in the passages I read to those businessmen—and notice, too, how natural it seems to you to act the same way they do! The fact is, the way Christ is asking us to live isn't natural. It's hard. That's why we need God's help to live that way.

If Jesus Had Never Lived

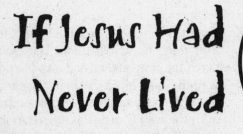

Dave

"I just can't get into Jesus," Mark said. We were at Young Life camp—I was his Young Life leader—and we were walking beside the lake.

"What do you mean?" I asked.

"Well—how do I know there even *was* such a person? Where's the proof? I read the Bible, about the things he did and said, and it seems like a storybook or something. It doesn't seem real. And anyway, it was such a long time ago; I don't see what it has to do with me here, today."

Mark isn't alone. A lot of people don't think Jesus, some guy who lived two thousand years ago, has anything at all to do with our lives now.

But the truth is that no one, alive or dead, has more to do with our lives now than Jesus. *Everything* about our lives would be different if Jesus had never lived.

Some things are obvious. We celebrate Christmas because that's the day we've chosen to celebrate his birth; we buy new clothes and exchange eggs and candy on Easter, the day he rose from the dead. We go to church on Sunday to worship him; obviously, we wouldn't if he'd never lived. We number our years from his birth: A.D. 1997 means 1997 *anno Domini* ("the year of our

Lord")—1,997 years after his birth. Many of us are named after his closest followers: Mark, Luke, Matthew, Paul, Philip, Andrew.

The religion established to worship him is the most widespread religion in the world, with more followers than any other.

But think a little deeper. What about slavery? Many of the people who opposed slavery were Christians, and they opposed it because it violated their Christian principles. Eventually they were successful in defeating the practice over most of the world.

John Newton was the captain of a slaving ship; he supervised the capture of Africans and carried them in his ship to America, where he sold them into slavery. Then he became a Christian, and suddenly his entire value system changed; he stopped trading in slaves and worked to outlaw slavery. Later he wrote the hymn "Amazing Grace."

Or what about rights for women? Many people think of Christianity as a system that tries to keep women in subjection to men, but that's neither accurate nor fair. "There is neither Jew nor Greek, slave nor free, male nor female, for you are all one in Christ Jesus," the Bible says in Galatians 3:28. Talk about equality! So not surprisingly, when the movement for women's rights began around the turn of the century, many of the activists were Christians who felt that men and women had equal privileges under Christ and therefore should have equal rights under the law.

We have child labor laws, protecting young children from having to work long hours under inhumane conditions, for the same reason.

So, then—many of the things you take for granted in the society around you, in the shape of your daily life, came about only because Jesus lived.

But think deeper yet. Jesus' life was not some accident. The Bible tells us that God sent Jesus, his only son, to die for us because our sins were so many and so bad that we could never make up for them. His sacrifice, his death on the cross, made up for our sins, allowing God to forgive us—a gift that we are free to either accept or reject, since God won't force us to accept his love.

And that is the greatest and deepest difference that Jesus makes in our lives. Without him, we would be completely separated from God, without any hope or possibility of ever bridging that great canyon between us to reach God, to be accepted and loved and forgiven by the most powerful and loving entity in all of existence, the one who created us. We would be lost—not just for this lifetime but for eternity, since our souls are eternal.

But because of Jesus, and Jesus alone, we can know God and be loved by him, now and for eternity.

If we choose to be.

Verse of the Day:

"For God so loved the world that he gave his one and only Son, that whoever believes in him shall not perish but have eternal life."

JOHN 3:16

Want to know More?

Here are some important things everyone should know about Jesus. First, as the verse above tells us, God loves us and wants us to spend eternity with him. But the wrong things we've done, our sins, stand in the way (Romans 3:23 and 6:23). Jesus died on the cross to pay the price for our sins so that God could forgive and accept us (Acts 10:43 and Ephesians 1:7–8). We receive that free gift of forgiveness and salvation by believing in Jesus and inviting him into our lives (John 1:12 and Revelation 3:20).

Just Do It:

What have you chosen? God gives us a choice of accepting Jesus' sacrifice on our behalf, of accepting God's free gift of salvation and forgiveness and eternal life, or of rejecting it. Maybe it's time that you said to God, "Yes, thank you, I want to become a follower of Jesus. I want to be loved and forgiven by you, Lord, and I know that this is only possible because Jesus died on the cross for my sins. I accept this free gift." If you haven't, and if you believe that Jesus died for you, then please repeat this little prayer or make up one like it, today. It's the most important thing you will ever say in your life.

And because it's so important, share it with someone else today. Talk to another Christian—a parent, a friend, a youth worker—and tell them what you've done. Share that happiness.

If you're already a Christian, then pray right now for all the students across the world who are reading these words today or will next week. Ask God to open their eyes so that they can see how much they need him. Pray that they will have the courage and the hunger to pray this little prayer.

What's a "Professional Christian"?

Dave

In the church youth group I grew up in, we heard it all the time. We heard it at camp, especially, on the last night when everyone was sitting around the campfire singing emotional songs (probably accompanied by one youth leader's out-of-tune guitar) and a few of the kids were getting up, wiping away their tears, and telling what God had done for them that week and how different they were going to be after this. Usually, at some point during the evening, the youth pastor would stand up and say something like, "Now while Joe plays through the chorus on his guitar, I want all of you who feel called to dedicate your lives to full-time Christian service to stand up and come down here to stand by the fire so we can pray for you."

Or maybe the youth pastor would take me aside one day, put his arm around my shoulders, and say, "Dave, I can really sense the calling of God on your life. I think you're headed for a life of full-time Christian service."

I think, though, that many of us in the youth group, including me, were a little unsure just what our leaders meant when they were talking about "full-time Christian service." Did that mean being a pastor? A missionary? A traveling evangelist? A Christian recording artist? All of the above?

Frankly, I think that *is* what they meant by it: someone whose "job" is to minister to other people in some way—someone, in other words, who makes a living at it, a professional Christian.

There's nothing wrong with that, of course. We need all the pastors, youth pastors, and missionaries we can get. But you don't have to be a pastor or a missionary to be in "full-time Christian service." Any Christian can do that. A clerk at McDonald's can be a full-time Christian. A housewife can dedicate herself completely to serving God. A high school or college student can be a full-time Christian, too.

What is a full-time Christian?

A full-time Christian is someone who realizes that their relationship with Jesus is the most important thing about them—more important than how rich they are or how they look or how talented they are, more important than how successful they'll be in their career or how well-known their family is.

A full-time Christian is someone who's willing to let God use them any way he sees fit—to just live the kind of life that people admire for its consistency and strength and honesty, to tell those around them about Jesus, or to be the kind of helpful, supporting friend that people come to when they have problems. Or for that matter, to go to Africa to spread the gospel, if that's what God wants.

A full-time Christian is someone who nurtures their relationship with God—spending time in prayer and reading the Bible, including God in every decision they make, talking with God casually throughout the day, considering how their actions and words might affect that relationship.

If you do those things, then you're in full-time Christian service, even if you don't get up into a pulpit every Sunday morning and preach a sermon.

Verse of the Day:

So whether you eat or drink or whatever you do, do it all for the glory of God.

1 CORINTHIANS 10:31

Want to know More?

Here are a couple more verses that tell us how important it is to live for Jesus in everything we do, every day of the week: Colossians 3:17 and 1 Peter 4:11.

Just Do It:

If you're like most of us, you go through most days (except for Sundays) without giving God more than an occasional guilty thought. Changing that habit might take time. Today take the first step.

It's a simple one, but it can be hard to carry out. Today keep up a running conversation with God. That's prayer, of course, but don't think of it as prayer. Just think of it as a conversation. Chat with him, as you would with a friend walking along beside you. (Silently, of course, unless you want your friends to think you've finally lost it.) Talk to him as you sit at your desk in class, as you eat, as you work at your after-school job or work out with your team, even as you watch TV. Ask him what he thinks of what's going on—you'll be amazed at how you can sense his answers to *that* question—or what you should do about certain situations. Tell him how much you appreciate the beauty of the clouds overhead, or the power of music, or the ability to taste your food.

If it starts to feel a little more natural to you by the end of the day, good! Maybe you should continue the experiment tomorrow—and the next day and the next, until it becomes a habit!

You're on your way to becoming a full-time Christian!

"Can You Spare Some Change, Mister?"

Dave

One afternoon Peter and John, two of the disciples, were headed into the temple where they worshiped. (That's right—it's Bible story time again. You'll find this one in Acts 3:1–10.) A crippled beggar—the Bible says that he'd been crippled since he was born—was sitting on the temple steps. He asked the two disciples if they could give him some money.

I hear this kind of thing all the time on downtown streets or outside airports or bus depots—"Can you spare a little change so I can get a meal, Mister?" I was coming out of a big Christian rally in the Georgia Dome in Atlanta the other day, and one enterprising beggar got a bright idea. He knew there'd be a lot of Christians there, so he tucked a Bible under his arm, and when he approached me, he said, "I'm a poor street preacher, brother, and I spend so much time out preaching the Word among the sinners that I haven't got time to work for my daily bread, and I'm about to starve!"

I wish I'd had the nerve to respond the way Peter and John did. First they told the beggar outside the temple, "Look at us!" So he did, figuring they were about to give him some money.

Then Peter said an amazing thing: "Silver or gold I do not have, but what I have I give you. In the name of Jesus Christ of Nazareth, walk." Walk? This man had been crippled all his life! How could he walk? Do you suppose he was filled with hope that Peter might heal him—or was he thinking something like, *This guy's wacko. I won't get any money out of him.*

Regardless of what the beggar was thinking, Peter reached out, took him by the hand, and helped him to his feet—and immediately the man's feet and ankles (the parts that had been crippled, apparently) became strong, and he began to walk!

Now what do you suppose he was thinking? *Whoa! Now I'll have to buy some shoes!*

Whatever he was thinking, it must have been something good, because the Bible says that he began not just to walk but to jump and to praise God, and he went with Peter and John into the temple.

There's more to the story. Peter got a chance to preach a sermon to all the people gathered around the healed man, and then the priests and others hauled Peter and John off to jail and later brought them before the authorities, and—but you can read all that for yourself in Acts chapters 3 and 4. We've already got to the part of the story I'm interested in today.

What were the first words out of Peter's mouth when the crippled man spoke to him? "Silver or gold I do not have." The fact was, neither Peter nor John had much of anything. They'd been wandering around for the past three years with Jesus; neither of them had a job, and like traveling evangelists, they'd been living on what other people gave them in the offering plate. And it's not as if they'd been lawyers or something before they started following Jesus, either; they'd been fishermen. The priests considered the two of them, in chapter 4, to be "unschooled, ordinary men." And they were. And penniless to boot.

So why did these two ex-fishermen act and speak so boldly, healing the crippled man (or to be more accurate, allowing God to heal him through them) and defying the authorities?

Because they knew that God can use anyone who's willing to be used, to do great things. Regardless of wealth. Regardless of how many years you've been to school. Regardless of how famous you're not. Regardless of age.

Did you get that last one? *Regardless of age.* A lot of young people don't feel that God can really use them yet in any big way. Maybe when they're older, with a college degree, a house, a nice car, a spouse—

But God used Peter and John without a college degree or a house or a nice car. In fact, they had nothing. Sure, they were older than you are—probably in their early thirties. But that's irrelevant. The fact is, they stood there before that crippled man that morning, with nothing but a willingness to be used by God.

The same thing you'd have had in the same situation.

Why wait till you're thirty and have a steady paycheck to be bold for God? Start now. "Silver or gold I do not have," Peter said. Odds are, neither do you—or to put it in modern terms, a walletful of bucks you do not have. "But what I have I give you," he went on to say, and you can do the same. A lot of energy. A strong faith in God. A passion for justice and good. A willingness to stand up for what's right, even if it's risky. Those things you have. And what you have, you can give.

And if you do, then—like Peter and John—you'll work miracles.

Verse of the Day:

"By faith in the name of Jesus, this man whom you see and know was made strong. It is Jesus' name and the faith that comes through him that has given this complete healing to him."

ACTS 3:16

Want to know More?

Read what happened after Peter and John were arrested, in Acts 4:1–31. This passage shows some of the secrets of their boldness.

Just Do It:

After you've read the story of Peter and John in Acts 4:1–31, as I suggested in the "Want to Know More" section, pray a special prayer for yourself, a prayer for boldness. Then start, today, forming the habit of looking for those times when you're faced with a choice: *Do I shrink back into the wallpaper and hope no one notices me, or do I step forward boldly, identify myself as a Christian, and take a stand?*

And when those times come, remember Peter and John and don't hide behind any excuses. Not even the excuse of your age.

Who's the Half Person?

Dwight L. Moody was an evangelist who lived about a hundred years ago. He was a colorful character, and there are a lot of stories told about him, but here's our favorite:

Dwight Moody preached at a small gathering one night and then got together with one of his friends afterward. "How'd it go tonight?" the friend asked. "Did you have a good response?"

Moody nodded. "Pretty good for a small crowd. There were two and a half people saved."

His friend grinned. "Two and a half? You mean two adults and a child?"

Moody shook his head. "No. Two children and an adult. The adult has already lived half his life; he only has half left to give to the Lord. But the children can give him their entire lives."

You may not *feel* like a child. You may feel as if you've been alive for hundreds of years and been through such difficult experiences that you've lost all of the innocence of childhood. But the children in Moody's day, before child labor laws and government agencies like Child Protective Services, didn't have such easy lives, either. And the fact remains that if you're still in your teens, you've probably got about eighty percent of your life still ahead of you, since most people in the U.S. live well into their seventies.

In other words, you're not the half person. You're the whole person.

Whatever God had in mind for you when he first thought you up, long before you were born—you can still do it! You haven't blown it yet!

And that is no small thing. One of the most common feelings adults experience is regret—regret that we didn't make better choices when we were young, that we frittered away our life without doing anything of importance, that we've already lived most of our life and lived it selfishly, and that it's too late to change all that.

But not you. You can hold your life out to God, whole and shining and unspoiled, and say, "Here. I want to do bold and exciting and important things for you. Sign me up." And he will.

God can use anyone anytime. If someone finally turns to him when they're dying of cancer at age eighty, God can still use them. But a *whole* life lived for him is better.

And you have a whole life ahead of you.

Verse of the Day:

Remember your Creator in the days of your youth.

ECCLESIASTES 12:1

Want to know More?

You'll find some great advice for how to do just what today's verse talks about, in Proverbs 3:1–5 and 4:20–27. (Note: "son" in these verses refers to young men or women.)

Just Do It:

With a whole life to live for God, how are you going to live it? What are you going to do? You want to know what God's will for your life is, of course. But it's OK to have dreams of your own of all the great things you'd like to accomplish for God. What's your dream? To be a servant of the sick and poor, like Mother Teresa? An entertainer or athlete who shares their testimony every chance they get? A groundbreaking missionary who explores unknown areas to find people who've never yet heard of Jesus, and then translates the Bible into their language? A wealthy businessperson who gives generously of his or her earnings to fund churches, relief efforts, and Christian organizations? A Christian artist or musician or writer who speaks the truth of God in a way that causes millions of people to understand its power?

All of those doors and many more are open to you. Take some time today just to dream—and to thank God that he reached you so young.

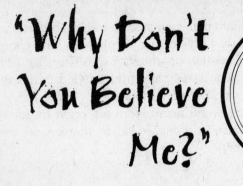

"Why Don't You Believe Me?"

Sarai

Wait a minute—is that name under the title "Sarai"? What happened to Ross and Dave? We're still around. But this next story is something that happened to Dave's daughter Sarai a few years ago when she was a sophomore in high school. (She's nineteen now.) We thought she should tell her own story.

I had just gotten home from school when I looked out the window and saw Brian, my boyfriend, riding his bike up the driveway. *Oh, great,* I sighed. I wasn't supposed to have boys over when my parents weren't home. In fact, I'd gotten in big trouble for that just the week before, and I'd said I wouldn't do it again. *And Eric will be home from school any second! I'd better tell Brian to leave.*

I walked out to the garage door and met Brian just as he was getting off his bike. "Hi," I said.

"Hi," he grinned.

"Look, I really wish you could stay, but my dad said—"

And just then the school bus pulled up in front of our house, and Eric, my little brother, got off and walked up to the house, looking at Brian wide-eyed as he passed. I glared at him. He would tell, I knew.

To make matters worse, Brian didn't really want to go, and it took me a while to convince him that I was serious. Finally he left.

Boy, did I hear about it that night! I tried to explain that I hadn't invited him over, that he hadn't even come inside, but my parents didn't believe me. We got into a big argument, and finally I yelled, "You guys don't believe me even when I'm telling the truth!"

It wasn't until months later, talking with my dad about that night, that I realized what I'd said. Of *course* they didn't believe me even when I was telling the truth! That's because I hadn't told them the truth about things in years!

I told lies to stay out of trouble. I told lies to protect myself and my friends. I told lies so that I could do things or go places that I knew my parents wouldn't give permission for if they knew what was really going on. And I got caught in enough of those lies that my parents knew I was a habitual liar.

To me it was simple: *THIS time I'm telling the truth! You're supposed to believe me when I tell the truth!* But to my parents, trying to sort out the occasional truth from all the lies was just too confusing. If I had lied about other things, why wouldn't I lie about this too? And how were they supposed to *know* which one was true and which one was a lie?

It looked very different to me at the time, of course. I figured, *I get in trouble whether I lie or tell the truth, so why not just have fun and lie about it?*

It took a long time to gain back their trust. Now instead of having a reputation for telling lies, I have a reputation for telling the truth. And I feel a whole lot better about that reputation!

Besides—telling lies about everything takes a lot of brainwork. You have to remember what story you told to who and when!

Verse of the Day:

A false witness will not go unpunished, and he who pours out lies will not go free.

PROVERBS 19:5

Want to know More?

Proverbs has a lot to say about telling lies. Check out these proverbs: 6:16–19; 11:9; 13:5; 20:17; 21:6; 26:18–19. And here are a couple of other good passages: Leviticus 19:11–12 and Ephesians 4:25, 29.

Just Do It:

Telling the truth is harder than we think. That's because we're often not aware of just how many times during the course of a day we "shade" the truth a little or exaggerate or keep quiet instead of admitting an embarrassing truth about ourselves. Most of the time, we do those things to make ourselves look better or to keep ourselves out of trouble.

Want to find out just how hard telling the truth is? That's your assignment for today: tell the whole truth—all the time.

The only exception would be that, as we all know, sometimes it's better not to tell an unnecessary truth if telling that truth would hurt someone—as when, for instance, your buddy shows you a picture of his unattractive girlfriend and, smiling proudly, asks, "What do you think?" The appropriate (and truthful) answer, obviously, is something like, "You're a lucky guy!" or "Wow! Some girl!" It would also be truthful to say that she's unattractive, but that would be unnecessary and unkind.

Be prepared: this exercise is going to be harder than you think. But you have a great deal to gain from forming the habit of always telling the truth. As Sarai learned, there are benefits in having a reputation for being truthful.

People will believe you.

Even when you're telling the truth.

The Laughing Jesus

Dave

I was sitting in church one Sunday morning, minding my own business, when the pastor slammed his fist down on the pulpit and woke me up. "It's time to get serious about Jesus!" he yelled.

I looked around at the rest of the congregation to see what they thought—and it looked as if they were serious enough already! In fact, we had just finished singing "I'm so Happy and Here's the Reason Why," but it looked as if they'd just finished singing "Man of Sorrows." Talk about sour faces.

Why is that? When the Bible talks about the fruit of the Spirit, in Galatians 5:22, it talks about love, joy, peace, kindness, goodness—*good* stuff. Stuff that should make us smile. So why do Christians' faces so often look like anger, selfishness, jealousy—the *bad* stuff the Bible talks about in Galatians 5:19–21?

Maybe *getting serious* about Jesus isn't the term we should be using. Sure, we should be "sold out" to Jesus, living for him one hundred percent. But *joyful* would be a more appropriate term than *serious*.

Listen to this story by Tony Campolo (from *The Church and the American Teenager* [Grand Rapids: Zondervan, 1989], p. 145):

> When my son Bart was just a little guy, I took him to Disneyland. After a wonderfully exhausting day of frontier

rides and space rides and jungle rides, I finally broke it to Bart that it was time to leave the Magic Kingdom. "Just one more ride on Space Mountain, Daddy," he begged. When I explained that we were out of time and money, he countered assuredly, "Jesus wants me to have one more ride."

How had he come to this glorious revelation, I asked him.

"Last Sunday when you were preaching," Bart replied, "you said that when we cry, he cries. Right?"

I agreed that he had indeed gotten the message right.

"Well," he went on, "doesn't it figure that if he feels what we feel, then when we're laughing and having a good time, he's enjoying himself, too?"

I had to agree with the logic of his argument.

"Then," he said triumphantly, "I think Jesus would enjoy me having one more ride on Space Mountain."

Not bad theology.

And it's a pretty good approach to life, too, as long as we remember that the Jesus in us is not going to enjoy doing something he has specifically forbidden us to do.

In Tony's story, Bart was using this principle to justify doing something that *he* wanted to enjoy. That's OK. But a greater application of that principle, I think, is to spur us to encourage joy in those around us. After all—the Bible tells us in today's verse that whatever we do for others, we do for him.

So next time someone tells you to get serious about Jesus, get joyful instead. Enjoy yourself and try to make sure that the people around you enjoy themselves, too. Smile. Laugh. Be a good friend.

Whatever you're feeling, whatever the people around you are feeling, Jesus is feeling, too. It really *is* Jesus laughing as he goes around Space Mountain one more time! (Jesus obviously wasn't enjoying himself much when my wife rode it, though. If Bart Campolo's theology is accurate, I think Jesus was terrified when my wife rode Space Mountain. I'm sure I heard him scream several times, and I think he almost threw up.)

Verse of the Day:

"I tell you the truth, whatever you did for one of the least of these brothers of mine, you did for me."

MATTHEW 25:40

Want to know More?

Read the entire parable from which today's verse is taken, in Matthew 25:31–46.

Just Do It:

Choose one person you know you'll be around today. (If you're reading this at night, choose to do this tomorrow.) Could be a friend or a family member or even someone you don't like very much. Resolve right now, before the day even starts, to treat that person as if they were Jesus—with kindness and compassion, trying to bring them joy, serving them gladly. Sound tough? You bet it is. But if you believe the Bible, anything you're doing for that person, you're doing for Jesus.

So try it for a day. Then remember this: that principle is true not just for today—it's true every day.

Growing Up in Jawbone Canyon

Dave

Jawbone Canyon.

A solid, rugged, western-sounding name for a solid, rugged, western place, a little-known semiwilderness on the desert side of the Sierras. Even then, back in the sixties, it wasn't easy to find any place in California where you could count on seeing only a few people and finding plenty of unspoiled land. That's why I liked Jawbone Canyon. Dirt roads wound through beautiful, deserty mountains, and every turn of the road revealed something new to explore: deserted ghost towns, beaver ponds, meadows full of deer, bobcats, mountain lions, and old log cabins that had once belonged to miners and were still in good enough shape to sleep in.

And I was there with one of my favorite exploring buddies, Steve. He and I had grown up together. We were halfway through college now, but since our early high school days, our favorite activity had been going out into the middle of nowhere and finding ways to risk death and injury to have a little fun. And we'd found plenty of ways: exploring old mines and caves, bodysurfing some of southern California's most dangerous beaches when the surf was high, catching rattlesnakes by hand, and the list goes on.

We'd managed to total out two cars by this time and give our parents plenty of gray hairs.

And this was a special trip. A last fling. Steve and I were each engaged to be married. Steve and his bride were scheduled to walk down the aisle two weeks after we got back, and my wedding was just two weeks after that. We knew we'd have few chances for this kind of guy thing after that, and we wanted to get in one last wahoo.

So in typical daredevil fashion, we were trying to lasso some of the range cattle that wandered semiwild through the canyon. We were on foot, so we had to be crafty—trying to drop the lasso around their necks from tree branches, for instance—but the steers proved craftier, and after an hour or so we dropped beneath a ponderosa pine, sweating and panting, and admitted defeat.

"Those cowboys earned their money, I think," Steve gasped.

"Hey, they had horses," I said. "If I had a horse—"

"If you had a horse, you'd break your neck," Steve said. "So. What do you want to do now?"

"Let's go check that out," I said, pointing to something I'd noticed while we were trying to rope the steers. It was an old mining area, just visible through the trees. A couple of tumbledown buildings, lots of piles of dirt from the excavation of the mine—and, as it turned out, a vertical mine shaft, dug straight down into the ground.

"What do you think?" I asked as we stood at the top, gazing down into the black pit.

Steve dropped a stone into the blackness. *Thump.* "Well, we know it has a bottom," he said. "I'd guess maybe forty feet down. There might be horizontal tunnels leading off from it."

"Or some neat old equipment down there," I added. We grinned at each other. "Let's give it a shot."

We tied one end of our rope around a nearby tree trunk and dropped the rest into the pit. Steve, the better scrambler of the two of us, grabbed the rope and headed over the lip of the tunnel. Slowly, testing the solidity of the rocks with his feet, he lowered himself until I couldn't really see his feet in the gloom—then he stopped and looked back at me.

It was a long and eloquent look. No words were exchanged, but both of us knew what the other was thinking. This wasn't the most dangerous stunt we'd ever pulled. But this time it was different. Not that we'd ever really thought, in any of our adventures, that we might really truly end up injured or killed. But even if we had, we'd have done it anyway. Somehow the risk of grieving our parents hadn't worried us like the concern that passed between us as I stood watching Steve gently rocking on that rope: *What would our fiancées feel if anything happened to us?*

Parents are past and present. But our upcoming marriages, the women to whom we had pledged ourselves, that was our *future.* And somehow that future held so much promised sweetness that the adrenaline rush of the moment seemed a poor trade-off.

Steve let his breath out slowly. "I don't really want to walk down that aisle with my leg in a cast," he said quietly. "You want to try it?"

I grinned and shook my head.

He grinned back. "Then, beam me up, Scotty." I grabbed the rope and helped him back up.

Yeah, we had a great trip. But we also behaved like people with something to lose. Something to protect. Because it was true. We had commitments, people depending on us. To risk life and limb unnecessarily would have been—a word that hadn't been in our vocabulary before this—*irresponsible.*

I don't think either of us realized what a major step toward adulthood we took that day. A sad step, in a way. But a necessary one.

Verse of the Day:

When I was a child, I talked like a child, I thought like a child, I reasoned like a child. When I became a man, I put childish ways behind me.

1 CORINTHIANS 13:11

Want to know More?

The Bible talks a lot about personal responsibility. Here's one good passage: Galatians 6:2–10.

Just Do It:

If you can get a few minutes of their time, ask one or both of your parents how they were different when they were kids from the way they are now. Ask them for some stories of things they did as kids, especially things they wouldn't have done as adults. Who knows—you might really get them to let their hair down and tell you some wild and woolly stories about things you'd never have guessed your parents were capable of. It'll help you to appreciate them more. And it might also help them remember what it's like to be a teenager.

Now ask yourself: In what ways are you different now than you were a year or two ago? In what ways will you have to be different in a few years than you are now?

Is This a Trick Question?

Ross

Iwant to tell you three stories, and then I have a question for you—and I'll warn you right now, it *is* a trick question.

The first story is about James, a twelve-year-old boy. His parents and teacher consider him easygoing, able to take things as they come. He gets along well with the other kids in seventh grade, just as he has usually got along with others before. One day, another boy accidentally knocks him down in the doorway to the cafeteria as he runs by. James jumps up, chases down the other boy, and attacks him with his fists, leaving a cut over the other boy's eye.

Everyone, teachers and other students alike, is shocked. This just isn't the way James behaves! But when the teachers check with his parents, they find out that James is coming down with the flu, is feverish, and has been unable to keep down anything he's eaten. James is sorry for hitting the other boy, and he apologizes.

Second story: Dan is fourteen years old, well liked by other students, and well regarded by his teachers. He has always been bright, and until recently he has had no problem keeping up with the other students. One day he has to confess to his math teacher that he's left his homework paper at home. She is mildly surprised, since Dan has never done that before, but hey—people make mistakes. So she tells him to bring it in the next day for half credit. She is even more surprised the next day when he claims to have lost his paper, and again the next day when he says that he has left it at home again. Comparing notes with Dan's English and science teachers, she discovers that this has become, very quickly and to everyone's surprise, a pattern with Dan. Soon the other students begin teasing Dan because of his "lousy memory," but the problem continues.

Third story: Sue, like Dan, is fourteen. She has always been a very verbal child who has no trouble making her feelings known— especially feelings of anger. Sue expresses that anger with great hostility, arguing with and complaining to her mother. Despite her love for Sue, eventually her mother loses her temper and yells at Sue. But that just makes Sue's behavior even worse, and she becomes even more hostile until her mother does one of two things: either gives in and gives Sue what she wants or overreacts with an even more intense anger and inflicts some serious punishment on Sue.

They both take a breather, but then something else will trigger Sue's anger, and the cycle will start all over again. "But that's OK," her mother wearily explains. "It's better than having her anger forced back down inside her because she can't express it."

Those are the three stories. Now the question: Is your expression of anger like that of one of those three kids?

Like that of James, who usually handles his anger well, but on occasion—especially when faced with unusual circumstances, like illness—is unable to control it, after which he feels contrite?

Like that of Dan, who doesn't even understand that he's feeling anger at all, but whose failure to complete his schoolwork is guaranteed to bother those authority figures—teachers and parents—who are the most likely targets of his anger?

Like that of Sue, who uses her anger as a way to manipulate and control the people around her, to get her way?

The answer: In all likelihood, there's some of each of those patterns of anger in you. (Remember, I *told* you it was a trick question!)

These are not the only three patterns of anger, of course. There are others. And anger in itself is universal; we all feel it, and we all express it in some ways. But some ways are more harmful than others. The "James" in all of us, for instance—the side of us that occasionally loses our temper over little things because we're tired or sick or under stress, and then feels bad about it afterward—doesn't usually cause much trouble for anyone.

But when you find yourself following Sue's pattern, *using* your anger to control people—making sure that the people around you (or maybe one person in particular) feel your displeasure enough that they will agree to do what you want, just to appease you— that's very dangerous. That kind of manipulation is one of the most destructive patterns in any relationship.

Dan's pattern is perhaps the most dangerous. He's not even aware that he feels anger, so he can't really talk to anyone about it or deal with it. Instead, it just shows up in negative behavioral patterns. But think about it: If Dan's response to his anger at his parents or his teachers is to get back at them by doing a lousy job, what's he going to do when he gets mad at his college professors? At his college football coach? At his boss when he starts working? That's right—he's going to respond by doing a lousy job as a way of getting back at those people, and then Dan will get kicked off the team or fired. In other words, in trying to hurt someone else because he is angry at them, he'll end up hurting himself most of all. Does that make any sense? Before you answer no, you should be aware that we all do this to some extent—and a certain, controllable amount of it is normal. But some people follow this pattern extensively in everything they do, and that is *not* normal— although it certainly is destructive. Psychologists even have a name for behavior like this: they call it passive-aggressive.

Do you see yourself at all in these three stories? Even if you don't, it's a safe bet that occasionally anger causes some problems for you. The important thing is to understand how destructive the way you handle your anger can be and to be willing to make some changes, if need be, to keep that destructive force from hurting you. Are you willing?

Verse of the Day:

"In your anger do not sin": Do not let the sun go down while you are still angry, and do not give the devil a foothold.

EPHESIANS 4:26–27

Want to know More?

Check out these other verses on anger: Proverbs 12:16; 14:29; 19:19; 21:19; 25:28; Titus 1:7; James 1:19.

Just Do It:

The problems that come to us from handling our anger poorly extend far into life and affect everything we do, from our jobs to our marriage. And once those patterns get set in adult life, they're very hard to get rid of.

Obviously, then, it's during your childhood and teen years that you want to learn how to handle your anger in less destructive ways. It's great if your parents understand that, because they can be a big help. But some parents don't realize that. Most parenting books don't talk about it, unfortunately.

So maybe it's time for a little talk with your parents. Ask them for a report card on your handling of anger. Ask them questions like: Do you ever notice that I'm handling anger in destructive ways? Does my anger ever cause problems around the house? Do you think that I'm angry more often than normal or that my anger is more intense than normal?

Then ask them to provide you with some guidance in your handling of anger—to point out to you when your response to anger is destructive, to help you choose more appropriate ways to respond. They'll be glad for the opportunity.

Following God into the Unknown

Dave

Have you ever been listening to an old, familiar Bible story—Jonah and the whale, Noah and the ark, Adam and Eve, Joshua and the Battle of Jericho—and heard something in it that you'd never noticed before, something that changed the whole story for you?

That's what happened to me a couple of years ago when I reread Daniel 3—the story of Shadrach, Meshach, and Abednego and the fiery furnace. You remember it: Shadrach, Meshach, and Abednego were Daniel's buddies, young men who conscientiously obeyed God even when it wasn't popular—in fact, even when it was against the law. And that's what they did when the king, Nebuchadnezzar (OK, let's face it—people had weird names back in those days), passed a law saying that everyone had to bow down and worship a huge golden statue he'd had made—a statue that looked suspiciously like Nebuchadnezzar. Shadrach, Meshach, and Abednego knew that this would be displeasing to God, so they didn't do it. Since they were the only three standing when everyone else bowed down, their disobedience was a little obvious, and the king ordered them arrested and thrown into a huge furnace.

I knew all that, so there really weren't any surprises—until I got down to verses 16 to 18 of Daniel 3, where Shadrach, Meshach, and Abednego answer the king, who has angrily ordered them one last time to bow down and worship his idol:

> "O Nebuchadnezzar, we do not need to defend our-
> selves before you in this matter. If we are thrown into the
> blazing furnace, the God we serve is able to save us from
> it, and he will rescue us from your hand, O king. But even
> if he does not, we want you to know, O king, that we will
> not serve your gods or worship the image of gold you
> have set up."

OK, that sounds—hey, wait a minute. What was that one line? "But even if he does not . . ." *But even if he does not?* Whoa! These guys are staring a fiery furnace in the face, are about to be thrown in, and they still don't know for sure what God's going to do?

I'd heard that story plenty of times, and somehow that little detail had always escaped me. I'd imagined the three guys standing there before the king, feeling smug, thinking, *Wait till old Nebuchadnezzar gets a load of what God's going to do here. He'll freak!*

It wasn't anything like that! Sure, they *hoped* God would save them, but they didn't have a hot line into God's mind any more than I do—or than you do. We don't know what God's going to do from minute to minute, and neither did Shadrach, Meshach, and Abednego.

I don't know about you, but for me that changes everything. Those three young men defied the king's law and allowed them-selves to be thrown into the furnace *without knowing how God would respond.* They obeyed God not because they knew he would save them from being burned to a crisp but because he is God and they had chosen to obey him even if it meant death—a rather unpleasant death at that.

Could I have done that?

I wish I could say yes.

But then, God has never yet asked me to obey him at the risk of being tossed into a furnace. At the risk of looking stupid to my friends? Yes. At the risk of having to deny my own desires? Yes. At the risk of having to confront coaches or teachers or bosses who were asking me to do things that I didn't think were honoring to God? Oh, yes. And sometimes even those minor risks have been enough to persuade me, with shame, to disobey God.

My level of Christian commitment would not have impressed Shadrach, Meshach, and Abednego.

It wouldn't have impressed Nebuchadnezzar either. But he was so impressed with the steadfastness of the three young men—and with the fact that God *did,* in the end, honor their obedience and save them from the furnace—that he said (in verse 28):

> "Praise be to the God of Shadrach, Meshach and Abednego, who has sent his angel and rescued his servants! They trusted in him and defied the king's command and were willing to give up their lives rather than serve or worship any god except their own God."

Looking for a worthy goal for your life? Here's one that's better than setting a world's record or making a million dollars or becoming Miss America. Set as a goal to have the kind of trust in God and obedience to him that makes people respond to your life as Nebuchadnezzar did to Shadrach, Meshach, and Abednego.

Verse of the Day:

Without faith it is impossible to please God, because anyone who comes to him must believe that he exists and that he rewards those who earnestly seek him.

HEBREWS 11:6

Want to know More?

Reread the whole story of Shadrach, Meshach, and Abednego, in Daniel 3:8–27. Extra credit if you skim chapters one and two and find out what their real names were before they were given those goofy ones.

Just Do It:

Take a few minutes to take stock of your life. Where are your areas of spiritual weakness? Is there a certain area—sexuality, honesty, popularity, family relationships, pride—where you seem to struggle with doing what you know God would want you to do? Think over the story of Shadrach, Meshach, and Abednego one more time; imagine yourself playing the part of one of those young men. Now think about your own situation again. Imagine yourself showing that same kind of strength and faith and trust in God that made heroes out of those three men. Now pray that God will help you to show just that kind of strength the next time your most difficult temptation occurs.

The
Revolutionary
Missionary

In the 1780s there was a young cobbler (that's a shoemaker) in England who was beginning to think that most of the preachers in England were pretty mixed up. His name was William Carey, and he would read passages of Scripture like, "Go and make disciples of all nations, baptizing them in the name of the Father and of the Son and of the Holy Spirit, and teaching them to obey everything I have commanded you" (Matthew 28:19–20), and he would wonder why none of the churches in England—or anywhere else, as far as he knew—were *doing* anything about it. Wasn't God telling us to go out into the whole world and try to convert the people there to Christianity? Then, why wasn't anyone going?

And to make matters worse, the preachers Carey heard seemed to be actually *opposed* to the idea of sending out missionaries. They felt that the instructions Christ gave to his disciples in Matthew 28:19–20 were meant only for the disciples themselves, not for those of us who came after them. In fact, when William Carey presented his ideas to one group of ministers, one of them said, "Young man, sit down. When God pleases to convert the heathen, he will do it without your aid or mine."

But William Carey didn't sit down. He was convinced that he was right—so convinced that despite his poverty (cobblers didn't make a lot of money), he took time out to write a book on missions, which won a few people over to his ideas. Then he founded a missions society. And finally, when he had enough financial support, he himself went to India as one of the first "modern" missionaries to be sent overseas.

That would be a neat story about bravery and perseverance if it ended there. But Carey's problems weren't over. He still had more critics than supporters, and the constant criticism back home in England caused many of his supporters to begin to doubt him. He even had to come back to England for a while to try to rebuild his support. Even within his own family, he didn't get much encouragement. In fact, his father said William was crazy, and his wife criticized everything he did.

Convinced that he was doing just what God wanted him to do, Carey stuck with it despite the criticism, and in the end he became known as the "Father of Modern Missions."

Are we telling you this story to try to recruit you to go to Africa as a missionary?

Yes! Sign right here on the dotted line, and then we'll . . .

No. We're telling you about William Carey because there are times in life when each of us will have to stand up for what we believe, even though everyone else—maybe even the people closest to us, maybe even other Christians—tells us we're wrong.

And then, like William Carey, we'll need to find the strength and confidence to do what we feel God wants us to do, rather than what the people around us are telling us to do.

And what can be harder than that? What can be harder than to stand up when everyone else is sitting down, to go left when everyone else is going right, to move when everyone else is keeping still?

It's one of the hardest—and most necessary—parts of being a Christian.

Verse of the Day:

"The one who sent me is with me; he has not left me alone, for I always do what pleases him."

JOHN 8:29

Want to know More?

Here's an exciting story of one godly man, standing alone, who did amazing things because he was willing to serve God even if there was no one else to stand with him: 1 Kings 18:16–46. Notice especially verse 22; it was one against four hundred and fifty! The secret, of course, is in today's verse, quoted above. When we serve God, we're NEVER alone!

Just Do It:

Try to find the chance today to talk to an older Christian, someone who's been doing this for a lot of years—maybe one of your parents, maybe a youth pastor. Ask them to tell you a story of a time when because of their faith, they had to do something different than everyone else around them. Ask them how it felt and how they found the strength to stand alone for what they believed.

How Much Sex Is Appropriate?

Ross

I know, I know—some of you, especially guys, are hoping that I'll answer that question by saying something like, "Two or three times a week seems appropriate."

But that isn't what I mean at all. Sex, you see, isn't restricted to having sexual intercourse with someone. Sex includes everything that has to do with the relationships between the two sexes, from thinking about the opposite sex to holding hands to going on dates—all the way up to (and including) sexual intercourse. (Notice that I'm talking about relationships between males and females here. Homosexuality is a whole different question.) *Sex,* then, includes a very wide range of activities and feelings. *Sexual intercourse* is just a small (but important) part of that larger area.

Remembering that can help you avoid some of life's worst problems.

Look at it this way. Almost all of us have strong sex drives. Some people respond to their sex drives by simply giving in to them. But that can cause major headaches for everyone involved: unwanted pregnancies, sexually transmitted disease, abortion, guilt, harm to our own development as well as the development of our sex partners, increased risk of cervical cancer, and the list goes on. Most of us have heard that list before. But here's a potential risk most people haven't thought of: the surest way to ruin a relationship is to have sexual intercourse with that person. You'll destroy trust between the two of you, as well as create a frightening array of fears, resentments, and dependencies that will destroy the positive feelings you once had.

(The one and only exception to this, of course, is making love to your spouse. It's strange but true that the very thing that has the power to drive two people apart before marriage becomes one of the most powerful ways to draw them together after marriage.)

So if you really like someone and want to continue to have a relationship with him or her, it's important to keep the "sex" in your relationship at an appropriate level—such as spending time together, sharing experiences and feelings, sharing appropriate and nonthreatening touches and kisses—rather than jumping into bed together and ruining the relationship forever.

Looking at my own life, at my children's lives, at the lives of my friends and of all of the people I've counseled over the years, I've never seen (or even heard of) a romantic relationship that was helped by premarital intercourse. And sadly, among those couples that marry after premarital intercourse, that inappropriate sex can even damage the relationship after marriage, sometimes even to the point of affecting their children.

I know it's hard to wait; believe me, I *know* how strong those sex drives are! But that waiting, as hard as it is, will one day come to an end. If you're smart, if you want the best for yourself and for your future spouse, you'll keep your body pure until the day you can give it—completely and without regrets—to your marriage partner.

Meanwhile, have good—but *appropriate*—sex!

Verse of the Day:

Finally, brothers, whatever is true, whatever is noble, whatever is right, whatever is pure, whatever is lovely, whatever is admirable—if anything is excellent or praise-worthy—think about such things.

PHILIPPIANS 4:8

Want to know More?

Here's a great passage that will help you keep your sexual desires in perspective: Colossians 3:1–17. (Remember: Your sexual side came from God, and there's nothing evil about it. But we can respond to those sexual desires in a sinful way.)

Just Do It:

"But I know I'll never be able to wait that long!" some of you may be saying. It's hard, I know. But sometimes we make it harder than we have to, by maintaining a vivid sexual fantasy life about our girlfriends or boyfriends, which just makes it that much easier to give in to the urges to do what you've thought about doing for months.

Play it smart. Control your thought life. Think about those things that will help the relationship, not hurt it. Do you love your boyfriend or girlfriend? Good. Then, you want what's best for him or her; you want to help and care for that person, not to ruin everything.

Memorize today's verse. Then, today, pay close attention to what you're thinking about the opposite sex. If it goes beyond the bounds of "appropriate sex," then rein those thoughts in, turn them in the direction of something helpful and positive in your relationship.

Can't do it? Ask some of your Christian friends to pray that you'll be able to keep yourself (including your thought life) pure, and promise to pray for them in the same way.

Is It Macho to Ask for Help?

Ross

A pilot was flying a small plane over the southern Rockies in New Mexico. The sun had gone down a half hour or so before, and the light was dying fast. He was flying into a bank of clouds, and a quick glance at one of his gauges told him that the outside temperature had gone down another five degrees.

If it goes down any more, he thought, *I'm going to have ice forming out there.* Ice formation on the outside of your aircraft is one of the greatest dangers in flying. It doesn't take much ice to bring a plane down. *Should I call Flight Watch?* the pilot wondered. Flight Watch is a network of flight service radio stations all across the country; it was formed to help pilots cope with weather problems. He thought it over—and then shrugged.

Nah, he thought. *I'll be OK. I don't actually see any ice forming yet.*

But within fifteen minutes, he did indeed notice ice forming on his windshield—and if it was forming there, then it was probably forming in other places, too. *I could call the nearest air traffic controller,* he thought. The air traffic controller would be able to help him chart out another course, or find another flight altitude, that would decrease the likelihood of ice formation.

But he kept his eye on the ice on the windshield, and five minutes later it didn't seem to have changed. *I think I'm OK,* he reassured himself. *As long as it doesn't get any worse . . .*

Twenty minutes later he noticed that the sound of his engine was changing noticeably and that his flight speed was decreasing. A quick visual check revealed the worst: ice had begun to form heavily, literally covering his wings, tail, and propeller. Panicking, he swirled the radio dial as he tried to locate an air traffic controller, shouting into the microphone. But by the time he had the air traffic controller on the radio, it was too late. Too heavy from its load of ice, his plane fell from the sky.

Yes, I made up that story, but I didn't have to—the history of aviation is full of stories of that identical thing happening to pilot after pilot. Why don't they ask for help sooner? Too proud to ask, maybe. Maybe they're afraid of getting into trouble with the FAA (Federal Aviation Authority) for flying in icing conditions irresponsibly and not getting out of that dangerous situation sooner. There are lots of reasons. But let's not be too hasty to condemn those pilots for their foolishness—after all, most of us live the same way they flew: we don't ask for help until it's too late.

Learning to ask for help when you need it—and when there's still time for it to do some good—is one of life's most important lessons and also one of the hardest to learn.

Ready for another of Dr. Campbell's little pearls of wisdom? Here it is: *There's no such thing as a stupid question.*

Sure, sometimes when you ask a question, it may *sound* stupid to you. Sometimes someone may even *say* that it's stupid. But even so, the best way to find out what's going on, to learn how to do something, or to understand something that's got you scratching your head is to ask.

And besides, it's in the Bible. That's right! God tells us that when we need wisdom, we should ask him. And who better to ask? God knows everything and is all-powerful. If he can't help us, who can?

Even Jesus asked for help. It's nothing to be ashamed of. It's never foolish to ask for help—in fact, only a fool never asks for help.

Asking for help on time is like putting oil in your car. It helps things go smoother, longer, and farther.

Verse of the Day:

If any of you lacks wisdom, he should ask God, who gives generously to all without finding fault, and it will be given to him.

JAMES 1:5

Want to know More?

One of the ways God helps us is through his Holy Spirit. Here are a few verses that tell some of the ways in which that happens: John 16:5–15; Acts 9:31; Ephesians 3:16.

Just Do It:

Make a list of all the questions you've been wondering about lately. And not just questions—list also problems that you need to solve but don't know how. List all of them that you can think of, even the embarrassing ones, even the ones that sound stupid to you. (Remember: *there's no such thing as a stupid question!*)

List, beside each question or problem, the name of someone you can ask for help or for an answer—or even someone you can ask to point you in the right direction.

Then—you know the next step. Ask!

Don't worry about sounding stupid. Actually, the more questions you ask, the better you get at it. You can learn to ask in ways that encourage the people you ask to give you better answers. Practice makes perfect!

Jot down, on your list, the answers or solutions you find by asking. See? And you might never have found those answers if you hadn't asked!

Some of your questions and problems, of course, are best presented to God. He's the only one who can answer some things. And he can handle any question—even the angry ones.

Need help? Get it! Just ask.

What's Integrity?

Ross

Want to hear a weird story?

I just read this in the newspaper. A dentist who had been arrested for molesting some of his female patients lost his license. So since he couldn't practice dentistry any more, he sued his insurance company for disability pay—a million dollars' worth! And how did he justify that suit? He claimed that since you'd have to be crazy to behave like that, his behavior must have resulted from mental illness! And therefore should be covered by his insurance!

Pretty crazy, huh?

But as weird as that sounds, that story is like a lot of things that are happening today. It's related, for instance, to things like this:

- In a recent book about the royal family, Prince Charles is quoted as saying that when he made his marriage vows to Princess Diana, he didn't really fully intend to keep them. (Isn't that sort of like saying, "I solemnly promise to be faithful to you—but please don't hold me to it"?)
- Several stockbrokers have been arrested lately for stealing the money—in some cases, someone's life savings—that had been entrusted to them to invest.
- A number of people who have become injured in accidents because they were driving drunk have sued the bars in which they got drunk, claiming that since the bartenders

could see that they were getting drunk, the bars shouldn't have continued to sell them liquor!

- The O. J. Simpson trial was a major fiasco, as we all know. Some of the star witnesses perjured themselves, which means they lied on the stand after taking an oath to tell the truth. And almost everyone who paid any attention to the trial, whether they believe O. J. was innocent or not, came away from it with their trust badly shaken in the police, lawyers, and the whole judicial system.

What do all of these problems have in common? They're symptoms of a crisis in today's world—a crisis of integrity. And what is integrity? Integrity is that quality of character that causes a person to:

- tell the truth
- keep his or her promises
- take responsibility for his or her personal behavior

When was the last time you heard anyone take full responsibility for a mistake they'd made? More often, we're pointing our finger in all directions, trying to find someone else to blame. And often our record isn't any better when it comes to telling the truth; many of us tend instead to say, true or not, whatever is most likely to get us the result we want—staying out of trouble, for instance. If what we say *isn't* true, that's called lying—but we don't like that word, so we don't think about it.

We hate it when people break their promises to us. But are we any better at keeping our own promises?

I'm not trying to cause a guilt trip here, even if it sounds like it. I'm just trying to point out that there's an important standard of character that few people in our society are trying to follow. When you find someone who *is* following that standard—someone who tells the truth, keeps his or her promises, and takes responsibility for his or her behavior rather than trying to pass the blame on to someone else—latch onto that person! That's a person of integrity, someone whose life you can pattern your own after.

Keep your eyes open for people of integrity. We all need heroes, and it's hard to find a better definition of *hero* than this:

a hero is someone who lives a life of integrity in a society that has forgotten what *integrity* means.

Verse of the Day:

The wise inherit honor, but fools he holds up to shame.

PROVERBS 3:35

The path of the righteous is like the first gleam of dawn, shining ever brighter till the full light of day. But the way of the wicked is like deep darkness; they do not know what makes them stumble.

PROVERBS 4:18–19

Want to know More?

The Bible tells us that we who are Christians are expected to exhibit higher integrity than others. Read Galatians 5:16–26.

Just Do It:

It's one thing to *find* a person of high integrity. It's another thing to *be* that person. Today keep track of your own integrity. Remind yourself of the three characteristics of high integrity. Then check yourself throughout the day. When you're tempted to "bend" the truth to your advantage—or to just abandon the truth altogether—how do you respond? Do you keep your promises today—in other words, can people count on you to do what you say you'll do? Do you try to shift blame onto other people for the things you yourself are responsible for?

Give yourself a report card at the end of the day; if you're keeping a journal or a diary, write it down.

Then do the same thing tomorrow. After all, being a person of integrity isn't something you turn off and on every now and then. It's something you work at every day until it simply becomes a habit.

And if you succeed, then the world needs more people like you.

Failing Forward

Ross

Have you ever read *The Screwtape Letters*, by C. S. Lewis? Great book. It's about two imaginary demons, Screwtape and his nephew Wormwood, who have been sent by Satan to tempt people on Earth and ruin their lives. The book consists of Screwtape's letters to Wormwood, offering advice on the best ways to tempt and deceive people. It's a very funny book—but it's also filled with wisdom about just how Satan does work to corrupt us.

And one of Satan's strategies, as revealed by Screwtape, is this: "Get Christians preoccupied with their failure. From then on the battle is won."

I hate to say it, but if Satan is trying to get me preoccupied with my failure, then he's doing a pretty good job!

I hate to fail! Don't you? Don't we all?

And one of the reasons we hate it so much is that it's hard to separate our feelings about our failure in one area of our life from our feelings about our life in general. In other words, when we fail at something, we feel as if our whole life is a failure. We feel as if we've got terminal failure disease. Our self-esteem goes down to zip, even if we've done well in other areas.

Which, when you stop and think about it, is probably one of the reasons Satan likes to see us preoccupied with our failures. It destroys our self-confidence and makes us think of ourselves as real losers—which is just what he wants to see! Besides that, it makes us fearful of trying again, because we're afraid we'll just fail again.

It's a funny thing, though—God never asks that we succeed at everything all of the time. He asks us to be willing to try the things he wants us to do, and to give it our best shot—but he doesn't insist that we succeed! It's normal to succeed sometimes and to fail sometimes. But we seem to impose higher standards on ourselves: we want to succeed all the time, and we kick ourselves every time we fail.

Maybe we need to realize that there are different ways to fail—and even that failure can be good! My friend Perry White, a pastor in Vicksburg, Mississippi, put it this way: When we learn from our failures, facing them honestly and trying to gain everything we can from them, then we are "failing forward." People who "fail forward" realize that failure happens to all of us, that we can't escape it, that it's nothing more than a normal part of life. We failed at some things yesterday, we fail at some things today—and like it or not, we'll fail at some things tomorrow too. Learning to accept that as part of the maturing and growing process is to learn to "fail forward."

Which direction do you fail?

Verse of the Day:

If the LORD delights in a man's way, he makes his steps firm; though he stumble, he will not fall, for the LORD upholds him with his hand.

PSALM 37:23–24

Want to know More?

Peter, as you may know, was one of the leaders of Jesus' disciples. After Jesus' crucifixion, Peter bravely took the gospel to many places, even though the authorities often arrested him and even threw him in jail repeatedly. But he was also a man who sometimes failed. Read of his greatest failure, in Mark 14:27–31 and 66–72.

Just Do It:

Your assignment for today: Find a copy of *The Screwtape Letters* by C. S. Lewis and start reading it! If you've already read it, then reread it; you'll be reminded of things you've forgotten about how Satan tries to undermine our faith and our growth as Christians.

Don't worry—it's not a long book and it's not hard reading. In fact, it's fun. I personally guarantee that you'll love it. In fact, you'll remember that book for the rest of your life. I promise.

I Love You with All My Kidney

Dave

In 1991 Michelle Stevens, a twenty-one-year-old from Washington, D.C., was told she would die if she didn't get a kidney transplant. She had spent eighteen months under intense treatment for her failing kidneys, but her condition was getting worse rather than better. She was spending three days each week hooked up to a kidney dialysis machine and was usually exhausted.

Her fourteen-year-old sister volunteered to donate a kidney, but she was too young, the doctors decided. Her brother said, at first, that he would give Michelle a kidney. But after he'd had time to think about the painful operation and the difficult seven-week recovery period, he backed out. Michelle's boyfriend, who had given her two diamond rings to show her how much he loved her, drew the line at giving her a kidney.

But Jermaine Washington, a twenty-three-year-old friend of Michelle's, had first his blood type and then his kidney tissue tested (a painful procedure in itself). When he found out that he was a perfect match with Michelle, he volunteered to give her one of his kidneys.

Michelle, though she desperately needed the kidney, wanted to make sure that her friend understood what he was getting into.

"I said, 'Jermaine, do you know how serious this is? I mean, this is really, really serious. We're talking about taking one of your organs out.'"

Jermaine talked to his mother, his minister, a hospital social worker, and a psychologist.

But in the end, he held to his decision. He donated one of his kidneys to Michelle. Why? "Her condition was getting worse, so I had to see if there was something I could do."

A simple reason: his friend was in pain, in need. A simple act: help her. But that simple act involved weeks of pain for Jermaine, not to mention increased risk in his own life: what would happen if, years from now, Jermaine's remaining kidney should be injured?

The word is *mercy*. Some people hearing this story would probably say, "He's quite a Good Samaritan." They'd be talking, of course, about the famous story that Jesus told about the traveler who found a stranger beaten and robbed, lying injured beside the road, and stopped (after several others had passed him by) to bind his wounds and give him water, and then carried him to an inn, where he could be cared for. (We list those verses below for you to read.) That too was an act of mercy.

When I was a Cub Scout, we were expected to do one good deed each day. And that, unfortunately, is how we've started to think about good deeds—as kid stuff, harmless but meaningless acts of kindness, beneath the dignity of a teenager or an adult. Jermaine Washington didn't think of it that way. Neither did the Samaritan. And fortunately for us, neither did Jesus Christ.

Because when you're in need, sometimes only a good deed—an act of mercy—can save you.

Verse of the Day:

But because of his great love for us, God, who is rich in mercy, made us alive with Christ even when we were dead in transgressions—it is by grace you have been saved.

EPHESIANS 2:4–5

Want to know More?

Read the story that Jesus told about the Good Samaritan, in Luke 10:25–37.

Just Do It:

Jermaine Washington showed mercy toward a friend. The Samaritan in the parable showed mercy toward a stranger—and yet we somehow have the feeling, after reading that story in Luke, that he'd have shown the same kindness to anyone: friend, stranger, or even an enemy. And that idea would have been even more clear to those who heard Jesus tell that story, because they'd have known that the man who was injured by the robbers was a Jew and that the Samaritans and the Jews didn't get along.

Today do a good deed—large or small, it doesn't matter. What matters is to find someone—friend, stranger, or enemy—who has a need and help them to fill that need.

Sound like Cub Scout stuff to you? Maybe. But most of us have the bad habit of getting so involved in our own concerns, our own desires, that we lose the ability to hear others calling for help. And it's only by consciously keeping our attention on the needs of others—as you'll be doing today—that we keep alive our ability to be compassionate, merciful people.

Les Misérables

In 1862 *Les Misérables* (pronounced "lay miz-air-OBB"), a novel by a Frenchman named Victor Hugo, was published, and it has since become a classic. Even if you've never read it, you may have seen the play based on that novel, or heard the music.

The story begins when Jean Valjean, newly released from prison, is tramping across the countryside and stops in the French town of Digne for the night. But he is unable to find food or a place to sleep, because of the distrust and hatred of the people, who know by the yellow registration papers he carries that he is a criminal. Finally he knocks on the door of a kindly bishop.

"'Look. My name is Jean Valjean,'" he says sullenly, hopelessly. "'I'm a convict on parole. I've done nineteen years in prison. They let me out four days ago. . . . I'm ready to pay, I don't care how much, I've got the money. I'm very tired, twelve leagues on foot, and I'm hungry. Will you let me stay?'"

In answer, the bishop turns and asks his housekeeper to set another place at the table.

But despite the bishop's kindness, Valjean wakes up in the night—unused to sleeping in such a comfortable bed—and finds himself unable to resist the temptation of all the valuable silverware he had seen during dinner. He argues with himself for an hour or so, then rises from his bed, steals the silver, and escapes out a window.

The bishop doesn't report the robbery, but the police routinely question Valjean when they see him sneaking out of town and, discovering the silver in his knapsack, they haul him back to the cathedral. To everyone's surprise, the kind bishop greets him enthusiastically: "'So here you are!... I'm delighted to see you. Had you forgotten that I gave you the candlesticks as well? They're silver like the rest, and worth a good two hundred francs.'"

The bishop then dismisses the puzzled gendarmes, places the candlesticks in Valjean's bag, and says quietly, "'Do not ... ever forget that you have promised me to use the money to make yourself an honest man.'"

Within twenty-four hours, Valjean finds himself on his knees, converted both to the Christian faith and to a lifestyle of honesty.

What brought about this remarkable change in a hardened criminal? A simple act of mercy. Valjean was used to being treated harshly and contemptuously; he had armed himself against that treatment. But he had no defenses against the kindly act of an old man.

And that's the way mercy is. It's deceptive. It's often interpreted as weakness rather than strength, but this "weakness" has the power to change lives.

What is mercy? It's been defined in many similar ways: as compassion for the needy, as forgiveness for the guilty, as reaching out to those who are helpless, as identifying with the miserable in their misery. Obviously, none of those come easily or naturally.

Still, as Christians, mercy is not simply an option for us—it's a necessity. We rely on God's mercy for our salvation. Jesus said, in today's "Want to Know More" section, that we should "be merciful, just as [our] Father is merciful" (Luke 6:36). And we're told in Micah 6:8 that what God requires of us is not so much to follow some set of rules and laws as "to act justly and to love mercy and to walk humbly with your God."

No wonder Jesus said, "Blessed are the merciful, for they will be shown mercy" (Matthew 5:7).

Verse of the Day:

"Love your enemies, do good to those who hate you, bless those who curse you, pray for those who mistreat you."

Luke 6:27–28

Want to know More?

Why not read the whole passage those verses are taken from? Jesus said these things in one of his famous talks—the Sermon on the Mount—right after he said, "Blessed are the merciful." Read Luke 6:27 through 36.

Just Do It:

It's one thing to believe that it's important for us Christians to show mercy. It's another to know just how to do that day by day. But we think today's verses give some hints. So, hard as it might be, think of one person who has mistreated you in some significant way—someone who, in other words, has acted like an enemy to you. Spend some time today praying for that person. And don't pray that God will strike them with lightning or give them cancer! Pray for their good. Pray that God will bless them, that he will touch them in some special way so that they will feel his love, that he will step into their life and make it easier, that he will draw them closer to him.

Now an even harder part: If you are around that person today, do something good for them. Maybe just a kind word and a smile (*that* will blow them away!), or maybe you can actually think of something nice to do for them. That *is*, after all, clearly what God is asking us to do in today's verses. So we can be sure that however hard it is, he'll give us the strength to do it.

And he'll be smiling.

Why Parents Say No

Ross

OK, raise your hand if your parents have never said no when you've asked them to let you do something.

What? No hands raised?

Well, that just confirms what we already knew. Parents say no. And most parents say no pretty often, especially during your teenage years, when you're asking to do a lot of things you've never asked to do before. In some families, the first time you ask to do *anything* is an automatic no. Once your parents get on a roll, they would probably say no if you asked to mow the lawn.

Being a parent, of course, I've had to look at it from the other side. When my child asks to do something new, should I say no? Or yes? And why?

When my daughter Carey was just starting her teenage years, she asked to go to a party. I called the home where the party would be held, and found out that it wasn't going to be a drunken orgy; no alcohol would be served, parents would be present. But it was definitely going to be a boy-girl party, with dancing, a number of older teens present, and probably several couples trying to find dark corners.

It was a tough decision. I had no real reason to doubt Carey's trustworthiness. She was, I felt, open and honest with her mother and me, and mature for her age. But that didn't mean she was mature enough to handle the kinds of pressures that might be put on her at that party, pressures she had probably never faced—at least in quite that intensity—before.

"Sorry, Sweetheart," I said. "I don't think it would be a good idea."

Her eyes flew open wide. "But, Dad—why not? You've never had to worry about me. I know what's right and what's wrong. Have I ever done anything so bad that you couldn't trust me?"

(Does any of this sound familiar yet? I'm sure most of you have lived through almost identical scenes with your own parents.)

"No," I had to admit. "You've always behaved very well."

"Then, why don't you trust me now?"

This was so hard to explain. "Carey," I said, "I *do* trust you. I'm very proud of you, in fact. You're just the daughter I've always wanted you to be; I wouldn't change a thing about you. It's just that—"

It's just that parents have lots of memories of their own—memories of times they thought they could handle the pressures or the temptations and found out that they couldn't. Memories of how high a price they had to pay when they blew it.

One of the memories running through my mind as Carey sat waiting for my answer was of a pastor I knew who often went into bars, claiming that he felt a calling to minister to the patrons of bars. Not long after that, his own life fell apart as he found himself caught in a cycle of behavior that destroyed both his ministry and his marriage. The temptations had simply proved too strong, despite his good intentions.

Does his failure—or your own parents' failures in the past—mean that you shouldn't be trusted in new situations? Not necessarily. But it does mean that parents are wise to be cautious; experience tells them that people aren't always ready to handle new pressures, just because they say they are.

But Carey was fidgeting, wanting her answer, with no idea where my feeble old mind had carried me. "Carey," I answered finally, "your good behavior gives me good reasons to trust you, just as I trust myself. But I also know that I can't necessarily handle any situation that comes up. And you too could easily find yourself in a situation that goes beyond your ability to handle. And I think there will be situations like that at this party. So just as I protect myself from situations that might prove too tempting, I'm protecting you in this case. The answer is still no."

She was, of course, upset. "You can't protect me forever, Dad," she whined.

How true. No parent can, and wise parents don't even try. But I could try to make sure that the temptations of adulthood came at her slowly enough, one at a time, that she would not be overwhelmed by the incredible number of decisions facing her as she moved from childhood to adulthood. And I could try to talk with her to strengthen her and prepare her to make those decisions—*her* decisions, not mine—when she would be forced by life to do so.

Parents have no guidebook that tells them when it's time to give their children the freedom to make certain decisions for themselves; parenthood is an instrument you play by ear. Sometimes parents give freedom too early, sometimes too late. We make mistakes. But we make those mistakes in the interest of helping our children grow into the independence that we know will be theirs someday.

Carey has her independence now—all she could want and more. She's a mom herself, having to decide when to say no. I think she's done a great job of moving into adulthood and making the right decisions (when I finally gave her the freedom to make them). I hope you do as well.

And that's why parents say no.

Verse of the Day:

Children, obey your parents in the Lord, for this is right.

EPHESIANS 6:1

Want to know More?

Here's a great passage from Proverbs that explains some of the reasons it's important to listen to your parents: Proverbs 6:20–23.

Just Do It:

Keep your eyes open, over the next few days, for a chance to discuss with your parents their reasons for saying no, and their feelings about your growing independence. But be careful—a whining "Why?" when they've said no is seen by most parents (with good reason) as a challenge to their authority. Instead, try an approach something like, "Dad, Mom, you've said no to my request, and I accept your answer; no it will be. But can we talk about your reasons? I'm not arguing; I just want to understand better your reasons for saying no. We all know that within a few years I'll be making those decisions for myself, so I'd like to know how you see that transition taking place."

Then however they respond, be sure you don't ruin the experience for both you and your parents by using this as an opportunity to argue or challenge. Listen respectfully, ask respectful questions. You may find that even in those instances in which you disagree with your parents' decisions, you'll be able to see that they were acting in what they felt was your best interest.

What's a "Magi"?

Back around 1900 there was a prisoner in the Ohio Penitentiary named William Sydney Porter. To pass the time in prison, he wrote stories. (Beats trying to teach cockroaches to dance.) When he got out of prison, he moved to New York and published his stories and became rich and famous—but not as William Sydney Porter. He published his stories under a pen name: O. Henry.

Many of his stories were really pretty famous; you've probably read some of them before or seen movies based on them.

In one of the most famous of O. Henry's short stories, "The Gift of the Magi," Della and Jim Young, poor, hardworking newlyweds in early-twentieth-century New York, want desperately to give each other nice gifts for Christmas. But they have no money. Nada. Zip. They have, in fact, only two valued possessions: Della's beautiful, knee-length hair and Jim's antique watch, which has been in his family for generations.

But on the day before Christmas, she makes the sacrifice: to buy a nice present for Jim, she sells her hair. Wait—she sells her *hair*? Yeah, that sounds pretty weird to us now, but in New York back then, there were shops where you could sell your hair so they could make things out of it. Embarrassed but with some money in her purse, she wraps her head in a scarf and runs off to buy Jim a beautiful platinum watch chain.

When he arrives home after work on Christmas Eve, Jim is shocked to find his wife's hair as short as a boy's. Suddenly Della is afraid she may have made a horrible mistake. Will Jim be so upset about her short hair that he won't enjoy the present she has bought for him? But Jim sees that she's frightened, and to explain his disappointment, he shows her the present he has bought for her: an expensive set of combs she has long wanted—useless now, of course, at least until her hair grows out.

But that doesn't reduce her excitement about her gift for Jim, and to salvage the evening, she brings it out: "Isn't it a dandy, Jim? I hunted all over town to find it. You'll have to look at the time a hundred times a day now. Give me your watch. I want to see how it looks on it."

Instead of obeying, Jim tumbles down on the couch and puts his hands under the back of his head and smiles.

"Dell," says he, "let's put our Christmas presents away and keep 'em a while. They're too nice to use just at present. I sold the watch to get the money to buy your combs."

Neat story. O. Henry loved those surprise endings. And of course, at the end Jim and Della are happier and more in love than ever, because they both know that for each other, they were willing to give up the things they loved most in the whole world.

Now to the question: Why did O. Henry call the story "The Gift of the Magi"? He doesn't even mention any magi. And what *is* a magi, anyway?

Maybe you already know the answer to that. The Magi were the wise men who traveled across the desert, following the star, to find the baby Jesus in Bethlehem. They brought him precious gifts: gold, frankincense, and myrrh. (Extra credit if you can tell me what those last two are.)

Next question: Why are we telling you a Christmas story when, in all likelihood, you aren't reading this at Christmas? This may be the middle of summer, and you may be sitting there in your bathing suit, about to head out for the beach.

Answer: Because the story of Della and Jim Young really is a pretty good example of the kind of gifts the Magi gave to the baby Jesus—gifts of great value that cost them a lot, possibly more than they could really afford—and also of the kind of gifts that we owe to Jesus today.

There's one big difference, of course. Della and Jim Young gave their precious gifts to *each other,* just as at Christmastime we usually give gifts to everyone—except the person whose birth we're celebrating. That's an odd birthday party, don't you think?

Maybe it's time we gave Jesus a belated birthday present. Like the widow who put her two little coins in the offering (in Mark 12:42) or like Della and Jim giving the only things of value they possessed, our response to Jesus should be to give him everything, just as he gave everything for us.

Verse of the Day:

Remember this: Whoever sows sparingly will also reap sparingly, and whoever sows generously will also reap generously. Each man should give what he has decided in his heart to give, not reluctantly or under compulsion, for God loves a cheerful giver.

2 CORINTHIANS 9:6–7

Want to know More?

Read about the widow and her two little coins, in Mark 12:41–44.

Just Do It:

Today think of a gift to give to God, one that you've never given him before. Maybe some talent that you have that you've never really dedicated to him, some behavior that needs to be cleaned up, or a relationship that needs to be brought under God's control. Then spend a few minutes in prayer, presenting that gift to him.

Happy birthday, Jesus! (Sorry your present's a bit late.)

The Frog Pond

Dave

Just a few blocks from my school, right next to the path I took to walk home, there was a hilly section with a lot of trees. It was fenced in with rusty wire, but that didn't stop my brother Ron and me. We found, hidden back behind the hill, down among some huge willow trees, the pond.

We weren't the first; there was already a makeshift raft pulled up on the bank to prove that other kids had been there before us. Trees, rocks, water, cattails, frogs, snakes—it was an unexpected paradise in a world composed almost entirely of streets, sidewalks, shopping centers, and houses crammed too close together.

Funny thing, though—my mom found out about the frog pond almost as soon as we did. How do parents know this stuff? And so almost before we had a neat place to go, we had a rule against going there.

"But why?" we whined. "We won't get hurt. Nobody cares if we go there."

"Then, why are there 'No Trespassing' signs up?"

How'd she know about that? "Those signs are *old*, Mom! They're all faded. Whoever put them up is probably dead by now."

"It's fenced, it has 'No Trespassing' signs, and it's dangerous. I don't want you going there. Period."

So the Lambert family established an official rule against visiting the frog pond. And Ron and Dave were good boys and obeyed the rule. For a month or so. And then the temptation became too great, and we snuck down on the way home from school one day, filled my lunch box with little frogs and toads, filled my thermos with tadpoles, had a great time crawling around on the rocks, and finally, reluctantly, walked the rest of the way home.

We were late, of course. So we made up some lie about a ball game we'd stayed for at school, and went back to our shared bedroom, feeling as though we'd pulled it off.

Until the bedroom door closed behind us and Ron gasped, grabbed my shoulder in panic, looked around frantically, and whispered, "My mitt!"

His mitt. His new baseball mitt. Which he'd just received for his birthday. Which we'd had when we'd gone to the frog pond but not when we got home.

He stood frozen for a moment, his face white, and then collapsed on his bed in tears. And being the sympathetic little brother that I was, I collapsed onto mine in tears, too.

"It's go-o-o-ne!" Ron wailed. "I'll never see it aga-a-a-ain."

"I kno-o-o-ow," I agreed.

"It was the best mitt I've ever ha-a-a-ad!"

"I kno-o-ow!"

Eventually my own weeping subsided, leaving only the sniffles, but Ron kept on, overcome with loss. Finally he blubbered, "I think we ought to tell her the truth."

Are you crazy? I thought, and I said, "OK."

"You go tell her," he wept. "And then just let all those frogs and toads and tadpoles go. Let them be happy, even if I can't be-e-e-e."

All those frogs and toads. "Ron?" I said.

"Wha-a-a-at?"

"I left my lunch box and thermos on the kitchen table."

But when, with fear and trembling, I'd made my way back down the hall to the kitchen, my lunch box was no longer sitting on the table. It was sitting in the sink, and my mother was standing in the middle of the kitchen, her hands clutched to her chest, and she was still gasping for air. Toads, of course, can't jump worth a darn. But those little frogs were jumping like champs, out of the sink, all over the counter, out onto the floor . . .

When I'd gathered them all, I came and stood before her, head down.

"We went to the frog pond," I confessed.

"*Did* you," she said.

I nodded. "We lied about the game. And we left Ron's new mitt at the pond." I dared to look partway up, about waist high. "He's real sad. Can I go back and get his mitt?"

She sat down. "No. You can't go back at all. I want you to never go there again."

"But what about Ron's mitt? Dad could go back with me—"

"No," she said, forcing me to look up into her eyes. "Ron's mitt is lost somewhere neither of you can go back to and get it. So it will have to stay lost. I'm sorry that it's lost. I know how badly he's been wanting that mitt, and it cost us a lot to buy it for him for his birthday. We can't afford to replace it. But you may not go back to get it."

I nodded my acceptance of this—wondering, of course, what other punishments they would decide on when Dad got home— and started back to my bedroom.

"Dave?" my mom said softly.

I turned.

"Disobedience always has its cost," she said.

It took me a long time, and a lot more disobedience, before I really figured out what she meant by that. The loss of Ron's mitt wasn't some punishment handed out by my parents for our disobedience. It was simply the natural cost of that disobedience. Like the boy who takes the car without permission and then wrecks it, like the girl who has sex "just one time" and then gets pregnant, disobedience always has a natural negative result. Not always an obvious one, but it has a cost just the same.

Except that, in Ron's case, that cost wasn't his mitt. One of his friends went back to the frog pond a day or two later, found Ron's mitt, and brought it back to him.

And I often wondered, as I watched Ron steamroll his way through his teenage years, accepting no law or rule but his own and suffering some terrible personal consequences of that disobedient life, whether it would not have been a kindness to Ron to let that mitt stay at the frog pond till it rotted.

Verse of the Day:

My son, keep your father's commands and do not forsake your mother's teaching. . . . For these commands are a lamp, this teaching is a light, and the corrections of discipline are the way to life.

PROVERBS 6:20, 23

Want to know More?

Read about the first disobedience and the incredible consequences, in Genesis 3:1–19.

Just Do It:

Pick a Christian friend, preferably one you've known for a while. Each of you try to remember three or four times you've deliberately disobeyed either your parents or the law or some other authority. Now, if disobedience always has a cost, what was the cost of each of those instances of disobedience? If you can't identify the cost, maybe your friend can help you see it. And remember: even when, like Ron, you seem to have escaped the immediate cost, there are always hidden costs that may not show up until much later.

"He Is No Fool . . ."

Dave

I can vividly remember hearing the news, even though I was only eight years old. Five missionaries had been killed by hostile tribesmen somewhere in South America. We didn't have a lot of details at first, but over the next weeks we got lots more, because the story captured the attention of America. *Life* magazine sent one of its best photojournalists, Cornell Capa, to record the story in pictures.

Eventually we learned that Jim Elliott, Nate Saint, Pete Fleming, Roger Youderian, and Ed McCully, five missionaries who had been trying to reach a virtually unknown and hostile tribe—the Aucas—in the jungles of Ecuador, had been murdered by that tribe on January 8, 1956, on a sandbar along the Curaray River, where the five had been waiting for days, hoping to make contact. All five were young men; all had wives and young children.

The photos published in *Life* threw the nation into mourning for the loss of these energetic and compassionate men. But the true story was not the deaths of the five missionaries. Missionaries had been killed before in trying to spread the gospel to remote, hostile areas; more have been killed since, and more will undoubtedly be killed in the future. No, the true story is what happened after the massacre: most of the widows of the five missionaries, with their children, stayed in Ecuador to continue trying to reach the Aucas with the gospel.

Think about that for a minute. If the word *enemy* doesn't apply to those who murder the members of your family, then the word has no meaning. The Aucas were the enemies of those women! And yet the widows still felt enough compassion to stay in Ecuador, at some risk to their own lives, to bring the love of God to their enemies.

The result? Within three years, most of the Aucas had been reached for Christ. And the Auca men who had killed the missionaries were playing with the slain men's children!

A tragic story with a happy ending. But it's more than that. It's a picture—drawn in red blood—of exactly what Jesus meant when he said, "Love your enemies."

It's a picture, too, of something Jim Elliott, one of the slain missionaries, said in his journal: "He is no fool who gives what he cannot keep to gain what he cannot lose."

Verse of the Day:

Do not be overcome by evil, but overcome evil with good.

ROMANS 12:21

Want to know More?

Read the entire passage we've taken today's verse from: Romans 12:14–21. A great pattern for how to live!

Just Do It:

"He is no fool who gives what he cannot keep to gain what he cannot lose."

A great thought, with more meaning than you'll be able to work through in a day. But make a start. Find some time to think about what Jim Elliott's statement means. What are the things you can't keep? Your life? True. We all die someday. Your wealth?

True again. You can't take it with you, as they say. Think of more things you can't keep.

Now—what are the things you can't lose?

Do you see why it's a good trade?

Winning the One Race That Matters

Dave

Adults are funny.

We have all these regrets—things we wish we hadn't done or wish we *had* done or wish we'd done differently. We're always saying things like, "If I had my life to live over again, I'd . . ."

And adults are very envious of teenagers. You still have the opportunity to do it right. We remember when *we* were in your shoes, and we remember how we blew it.

One of the things I regret is my performance in track in high school. I was a pretty decent runner—good enough that in my events, I usually qualified for the city meet and the league finals. And most years, I ran well enough in the league finals to qualify for the district finals.

But the truth is, I got that far without really working very hard at conditioning and preparation. I was an above-average runner who was satisfied to expend an average amount of effort. So I would get to the district finals, take one look at the runners I would be competing against, notice their muscle tone, read their list of winning times, and think, "I'm never gonna beat these guys." And of course, I wouldn't.

Thirty years later, looking back on that time, I feel a stinging regret that I didn't push myself, expend a maximum amount of effort, not only in my races but also in conditioning, just to see how far I could go, how fast I could get. Could I have beaten those guys at districts if I'd been working as hard as they were? Maybe. But now I'll never know. You get one shot at those things, and you either give it all you've got or miss that chance forever.

I think of that when I read certain passages of the Bible that point out that the Christian life is a lot like an athletic event. In 1 Corinthians 9:24–27, Paul asked,

> Do you not know that in a race all the runners run, but only one gets the prize? Run in such a way as to get the prize. Everyone who competes in the games goes into strict training. They do it to get a crown that will not last; but we do it to get a crown that will last forever. Therefore I do not run like a man running aimlessly; I do not fight like a man beating the air. No, I beat my body and make it my slave so that after I have preached to others, I myself will not be disqualified for the prize.

I like that part about competing "to get a crown that will last forever." I won a lot of medals and ribbons in track in high school. Where are they now? I don't even know. Some of them I gave to girls I dated, and when we broke up, I never got them back. Others have just disappeared over the years. But the prize we strive to win in the Christian life we will never lose, and it can never be taken away from us. And it lasts forever. Forever.

I guess I'm grateful for my high school athletic experience, even though I never reached my true potential. It was a good lesson—a reminder that in the contest that really matters, I need to give it everything I've got. I need to be able to say, as Paul said in 2 Timothy 4:7, "I have fought the good fight, I have finished the race, I have kept the faith."

I want to be able to say that, too—so that someday I can hear God say, "Well done, good and faithful servant!. . . Come and share your master's happiness!" (Matthew 25:23).

Verse of the Day:

Therefore, since we are surrounded by such a great cloud of witnesses, let us throw off everything that hinders and the sin that so easily entangles, and let us run with perseverance the race marked out for us. Let us fix our eyes on Jesus, the author and perfecter of our faith, who for the joy set before him endured the cross, scorning its shame, and sat down at the right hand of the throne of God. Consider him who endured such opposition from sinful men, so that you will not grow weary and lose heart.

HEBREWS 12:1–3

Want to know More?

Ready to hear some pretty bold and plain words about the discipline it takes to win the race? Read Hebrews 12:4–13. Are you tough enough to take it?

Just Do It:

You've finished this book. We have so much more we wish we could say, but we're out of room. So it seems appropriate to end with a challenge to live your life as if being a Christian matters more than anything else on earth—which, of course, it does. And that is exactly what those verses we've quoted today are telling us: "Let us throw off everything that hinders and the sin that so easily entangles, and let us run with perseverance the race marked out for us."

Both of us, Ross and Dave, thank you for letting us share some thoughts and some time with you over the past weeks. But where do you go from here? What changes will you make in your life and your habits and your attitudes, in order to "fight the good fight"?

Make today a day of commitment and decision. Commit to throw yourself into serving God with the same single-minded dedication and effort that a top athlete puts into competing in his sport. Pray a prayer of commitment and ask for God's help in keeping your end of the bargain. Then make some decisions: How will your life have to change to make that happen? What specific steps do you need to take—regarding such habits as Bible reading and prayer and church attendance or how you spend your time or who you hang around with and what you talk about—to stick with your new commitment?

The two of us are behind you all the way, with our encouragement and with our prayers. You can do it—not in your own power but with the power of the Holy Spirit that God gave to you when you became a Christian.

Claim that power. Be bold! Be strong!

Now . . .

On your mark . . .

Get set . . .

We want to hear from you. Please send your comments about this
book to us in care of the address below. Thank you.

ZondervanPublishingHouse
Grand Rapids, Michigan 49530
http://www.zondervan.com